The Story-Teller's Guide to

Wedding Photography

Rachel Raburn

The Story-Teller's Guide to

Wedding Photography

How to Start, Market and Grow Your Business

Photographs by Rachel Raburn

This book is dedicated to my parents, Bob and Patty, for their endless support, encouragement, and buying me my first camera. I wouldn't be the person I am today without their love.

And to my husband Mark, who bought me my first DSLR and walks with me as I become the person I will be tomorrow.

Preface

This is the book I wish I could have read before I started my own wedding photography business! All of this information was gathered over 18 months of research with lots of trial and error as I put it into practice. I didn't find all of it in one easy-to-read location, and I had to learn quite a few of these lessons the hard way.

In taking the time to write down everything I learned, I'm hoping to save you the trouble and headache of doing it the way I did. This book will help you start your own photography business, with lots of helpful tips and the best websites to use each step of the way.

I wrote this with a certain type of photographer in mind: the one who doesn't want to create the same cookie cutter pictures of posed groups that every bride has stashed away on a CD. You're reading this because you want to take story-telling pictures, the kind that capture the emotions and memories that each couple can look back on as precious treasures for the rest of their lives. You want to create finished pieces of art, in albums and as wall art, for your clients.

The style I use is actually a blend of old and new. I focus on the events and emotions of the day, and also make sure to get the posed family shots that family members of the bride and groom will want. This gives me a combination that's the best of both worlds.

Starting a photography business is a lot like having a baby. You may have seen other friends start their own businesses, and you've wanted one of your own for a few years. Now you feel like it's time to make it happen. How hard could it be? Your friends may make it look easy, but you don't see all the worry, stress, headaches, loss of sleep and frustration that goes on behind the scenes. They'll tell you it's worth it, but the only way to find out is to take the plunge and do it yourself!

When I first gathered up the courage to start my business, I was inspired by a quote that I still come back to again and again.

"You cannot fail unless you stop trying".

Starting any kind of business is scary. Your head is full of "what-ifs" and worst-case scenarios. The worst fear of all for me was the fear of failure.

When I heard that quote it literally changed my entire perspective. The only way I could fail was if I quit. Gave up. Stopped trying. All I had to do was commit myself 100% to *never* stop trying, and I would never fail.

You will find success with your business as well, as long as you don't give up!

So let's get started with this amazing adventure!

Contents

Note: Since this book is about starting your own business, I chose to use mostly photos that I took during my first year shooting weddings. They aren't all my best images, but they're the ones I felt would best illustrate the lessons in each chapter!

Chapter One

Before You Get Started

--Taking Inventory--

One of the best things about choosing wedding photography as your business is the low start-up cost. You don't need an office or studio, or all those expensive studio lights and props.

I started my business with a basic Canon DSLR, the Rebel T3i. I had the kit lens, an 18-55mm, as well as an inexpensive 70-300mm lens. That's it! I didn't even have an off-camera flash.

The very first wedding I shot, there were guests at the wedding with much nicer camera gear than I was using. Talk about a blow to my ego! However, I had the skill and artistic vision (and a lot of confidence!) that enabled me to succeed, and the bride was beyond thrilled with the images I gave her.

So you really can start with almost nothing, although I wouldn't recommend doing it with quite the bare-bones set up that I had!

But just for the sake of argument, let's look at what you absolutely must have to successfully shoot a wedding: A camera (preferably a DSLR), a lens, a computer with software that will let you develop your RAW images (more on that later), an internet connection, skill, lots of patience, and a boatload of confidence!

Don't let a small budget stop you. You really don't need to buy that top-of-the-line full frame camera and name brand lenses to get started. Buy what you can afford, and work your way up. Set aside some of your profit toward a nicer camera, and upgrade as you go.

There's another benefit to this as well: you'll develop skills without even realizing it! You have to work twice as hard to create outstanding images using your basic gear, and you'll need to learn how to use those settings – no more shooting in automatic!

To get the most out of your camera, you'll have to learn good composition, find (or create) ideal lighting, and use every method in your power to get those shots.

But the payoff will come when you get to upgrade, and you realize how much more you can do with even better equipment. You'll have the skills you need to make the most of the higher-grade gear, and it will pay off with amazing results!

Another option I highly recommend is renting. For the first 6 or 7 weddings that I shot, I rented a second camera body and a nice lens. This has several benefits. First, it lets you try out different cameras that are newer and fancier than the one you own. This will help you decide which one you eventually want to upgrade to.

Second, you really should have two camera bodies when shooting a wedding, even as a beginner. That gives you a backup in case something goes wrong. It also goes much more smoothly if you have two different lenses and don't have to keep switching them back and forth. Just grab the other camera that's hanging off the other shoulder (or from your assistant) and keep shooting.

Of course, you want to rent this nicer fancier camera well in advance of the wedding, so you have plenty of time to become familiar with it. You don't want to show up at a wedding and spend the first 30 minutes trying to figure out how to set your exposure compensation, or switch to spot metering!

The company I always use for my rentals is Borrowlenses.com. They have excellent customer service and I've never had any problems with the cameras I've used. Just make sure you read the description of each camera you rent, and make sure that you also select lenses that are compatible with it.

You may need a different kind of memory card as well, if you're renting a newer camera. I once decided to rent a Canon 5d Mark ii, and find out for myself if having a full frame really made all the difference I'd read about. (It does, by the way!)

I didn't get the camera and lens in the mail until the afternoon of the day before the wedding (my first mistake!). I didn't actually open the box and start getting ready until late in the day. I figured I had plenty of time to play with the settings and get used to using it.

Imagine my horror when I realized it took a completely different memory card (CF) from the ones I had (SD), and the nearest stores in our small rural town didn't have any in stock. I began to panic, until my husband saved the day by finding one in the next town.

I ended up with very little time the next morning to become familiar with the camera. During the wedding I know I didn't have the settings quite the way I needed them. In spite of the panic under the surface, I projected nothing but calm confidence. And I worked twice as hard as I ever had before to get some amazing shots. It was enough to let me see what kind of potential that camera had, even in the hands of a person who didn't know quite how to use it!

That wedding became one of my favorites, and some of those images are still in my portfolio.

Now that you know you probably already have the gear you need to get started, let's talk about the other things I mentioned: skill, patience and confidence.

Skill is definitely a must for a wedding photographer. If you don't already know how to use your camera and get great results, please practice on your own family and friends before agreeing to shoot a wedding! A wedding is a one-time event, and there are no do-overs if you mess up.

That fact is actually why I decided to start shooting weddings. For my own wedding in 2002, we were on a very tight budget. I mean, DIY decorations and flowers from our neighbor and sewing my own wedding gown kind of tight. We naturally looked around for the right photographer for our needs (cheap). And we found one: a local lady who only charged $400. She showed us an album with a few nice pictures in it, and we happily paid our 50% deposit.

What happened at our wedding was really heart breaking. But now that I'm in the business myself, I can appreciate how horrible the poor lady must have felt.

She didn't get any pictures of me and my father walking down the aisle, because she had run out of film and was reloading. (Remember, this was before digital!) She missed the recessional when my husband and I walked out together, because she didn't get moved to the end of the aisle in time. She actually got there just as we did, and waved frantically for us to go back and do it again!

When my mother and I arrived at her home weeks later to pick up the prints and pay her the remaining $200, she greeted us with this statement: "I decided to give you a discount, since some of the pictures came out a little blurry."

That was putting it mildly. They all looked as if they'd been taken through a grainy grey filter. They were terrible! She told us she'd ben "experimenting with a new flash".

So I don't have any wedding pictures. Not any that I'd want to put on my wall, anyway. There are a few decent ones that various guests took, and those are the few that I kept.

Now you know why I wanted to become a wedding photographer. I want to keep that kind of nightmare from happening to another bride, ever again!

--Portfolio Building—

So you have your gear, and you have the skill to use it well. Next up is patience. Why patience? Because even though you have the gear and the skills, you won't have weddings just fall into your lap. Getting your business "out there" and getting jobs can be a slow process.

It will take even longer than you may have hoped for if you follow my advice. But remember that a baby takes nine months! You can give yourself plenty of time to start your business too, and it'll be worth it, I promise!

Before you start advertising and taking deposits, there are two things you should do. The first one is to find an established wedding photographer who will let you shadow them. Don't even bring a camera. Just watch what they do, how the timeline works, how they wrangle guests for the group shots and deal with that annoying groomsman who keeps offering suggestions on how to do their job.

You can offer to carry gear, and just be helpful. For free, of course. You're getting an amazing education, so be grateful!

After this experience, if you still want to get into the business, try being a second shooter. You'll get more of a taste for the job, without the stress of having the full responsibility on your shoulders. Keep in mind that any pictures you take will belong to the head photographer, and his or her business.

When you're just starting out, you might have to be willing to second shoot for free. Once your main photographer has gained confidence in your abilities you can expect to be compensated based on the going rate in your area. I pay my second shooter $30 per hour, and allow her to use the pictures she takes in her portfolio. Not every photographer will allow you to use the pictures you take, so make sure you both sign a contract that clearly outlines the terms you've agreed to.

Once you've tagged along and shared in the stress and sore feet of a few weddings, you can move on to step two. Actually, you can work on both at the same time! The second thing is portfolio building.

You may wonder how you can have a portfolio of wedding pictures when you haven't shot any weddings. But you might be surprised just how much you can do! When I got started, I came up with a list of wedding-related things that I could shoot at home. This is where my artistic and crafting skills came in handy!

I went to thrift shops a lot. I bought sparkly and sequined things to use as backdrops for detail shots of rings. (I shot those using my own wedding ring, and a collection of costume jewelry that I bought on eBay.)

One of my favorite detail shots was one I took with a cheap ring and a set of gold sequined waste baskets!

I also bought a wedding gown at Goodwill for $12 that was my sister-in-law's size, and asked her to pose for some bridal shots. You could ask around for friends and family members who might be willing to put on their gowns and pose for you! (More on modelling calls later.)

You could borrow a wedding dress to take close-up shots of the lace or beadwork, hang it in a window or from a wide doorway for that iconic dress shot, or drape it over a chair or bed with a sparkly pair of shoes and a veil.

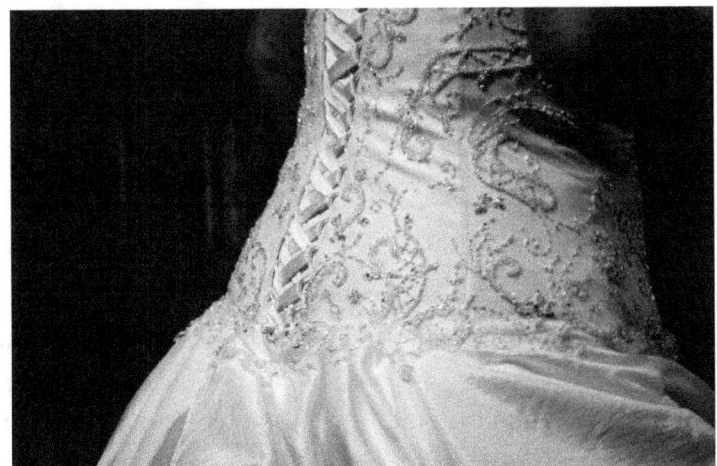

I also got creative and designed a wedding invitation, place cards and table numbers for a fake wedding. (This is also referred to as a 'stylized shoot'.) Most computers have some kind of basic program that you can use for this. I printed them out, added some ribbon, and them gathered some nice dishes and set up a reception table.

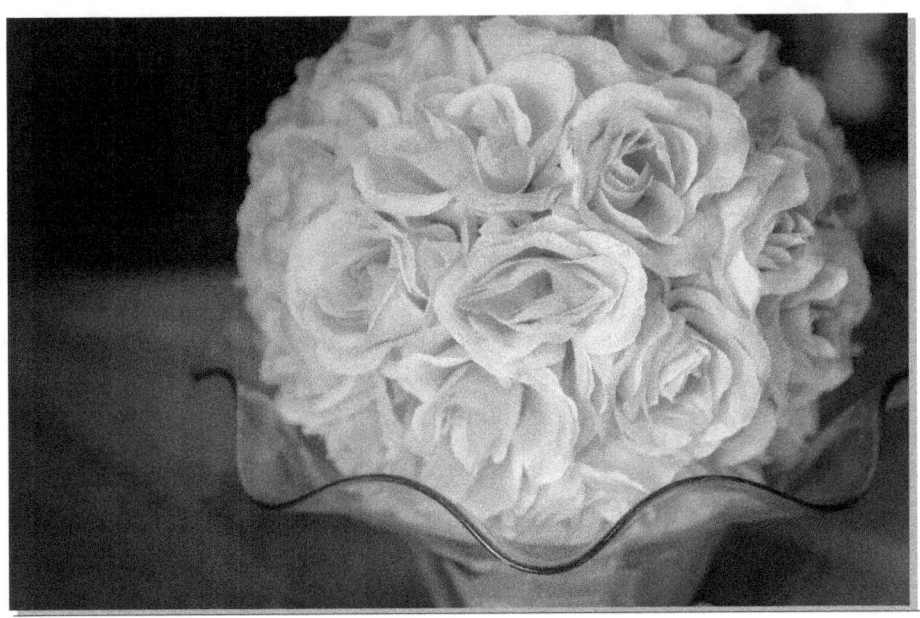

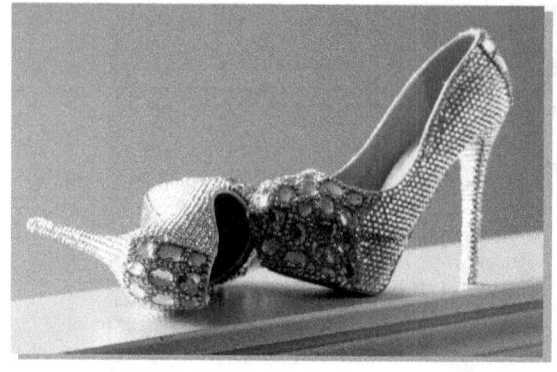

I started with two sawhorses and a wide board, and set it up outside in a shady spot. I added a lace tablecloth, lovely cloth napkins, china, silver and some beautiful turquoise water glasses. I even scrounged around my house for items to make into a centerpiece with a cottage chic theme. When it was finished, I was thrilled! It was lovely and elegant, and I was able to get some perfect shots of what looked like an outdoor reception.

Something else that's easy to find is flowers. Think of setting a pretty chair by a window with good lighting, and placing a bouquet of fresh flowers on it.

Be creative! There are lots of ways to build your portfolio without shooting a wedding. You may even have taken pictures already that have a romantic feel to them, or would fit the style you're trying to pull together.

I actually booked three weddings from my initial portfolio, before I had a single image from a real wedding on my website. One client told me he really liked my style, and the emotion that my photos conveyed. Your future clients should be able to see your unique style and skill based on your early portfolio.

Let's look at the idea of a modelling call a bit more. In a model release form the model agrees to let you take pictures of them that you are free to use for any kind of promotion or marketing. In exchange, they are offered compensation of some kind. This can be an 8x10 print, or a CD of a few watermarked images for their use in a modelling portfolio.

You can try putting the word out on Facebook that you're looking for models for a stylized photo shoot. You can ask for couples, or ladies only, depending on what you want to shoot. Ask for anyone who's interested to message you or send an email. Lots of people would be thrilled to get a photo session for free!

--A Shot of Confidence—

Once you've assisted at several weddings and built up your portfolio, you're almost ready to hang up your shingle. Confidence is the final ingredient, and you'll need plenty!

I'm naturally a quiet person, and would rather sit in a cozy recliner with a good book and a cup of coffee than any social situation you could name. I'm not shy, I'm just not socially inclined! But in this business you have to have people skills. I had to really push myself the first year, to get comfortable with directing strangers and acting like I knew what I was doing. You need to be a leader, give direction to your assistant, and be able to give clear instructions to others for posing. You also have to believe that you have what it takes to do your job. If you walk into a room projecting calm confidence, you'll convince everyone else too!

At the second wedding I shot, the reception was indoors in the evening. The room was very dark, except for the dance floor which was flashing with multi-colored lights. I had rented a Speedlight for that wedding, but didn't know very much about lighting a reception. I thought one flash mounted on my camera would be fine, but I quickly found out I was wrong.

As the bride and groom shared their first dance, then danced with their father/mother, I was pretty close to a panic attack! The camera's automatic focus couldn't work well in that lighting, and the shots that I did get were blurry or dark. I didn't know what to do, and my heart was pounding.

But outwardly, I was cool as ice. I chatted with the father of the bride when he came over to watch me, and moved around the room taking pictures from different angles. I was sweating and freaking out inside, but nobody else ever knew that. In fact, one of the reviews I got from that wedding mentioned how calm and relaxed I was the whole time!

Thankfully, I was able to salvage enough from that dance to make some artistic black and white photos that looked like I'd used motion blur on purpose to show movement. The bride and groom loved them!

I've learned a lot from my early experiences, but that doesn't mean shooting weddings is now stress-free! In fact, there's pretty much constant stress. The bride will be running late, and that pushes back your entire timeline so you have to rush. Then there will be shots the mother-in-law requests, and there's always one family member who will be MIA when the time comes for the group shots.

You may have a flash die, a memory card crash, a lens malfunction, or a shutter jam. (Thankfully, you brought backups of everything, right?)

You may have unruly guests, loud music pounding into your head, foot and leg cramps for standing for 5 hours straight, and your camera feels like it weighs eight pounds.

But you are the wedding photographer! You're a pro, and you know what you're doing. You will smile, and project a polite and charming attitude at all times. You'll assure the bride that everything is perfect, she's more beautiful than she can imagine, and the whole day has been amazing.

That's what confidence can do for you. It's believing in your own abilities, and bringing a calm presence with you everywhere you go.

You can never complain out loud about "bad light" or show confusion over your settings. You can't hesitate when asked by someone "where should I stand?"

People will usually listen to the person who looks, acts and feels like they're in charge. That person needs to be you!

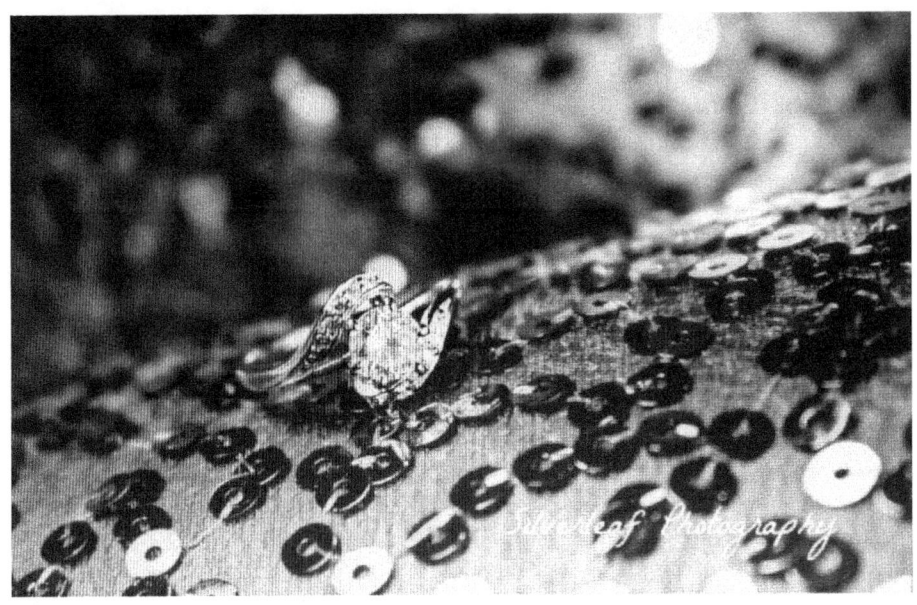

This is that image with the ring I bought on eBay and the sequined wastebaskets.

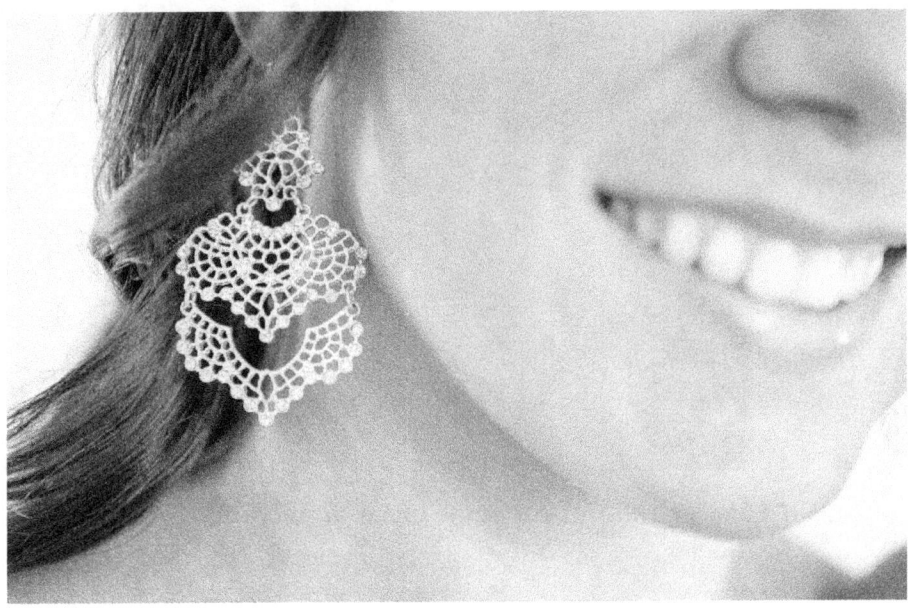

Any elegant jewelry can be used for portfolio images.

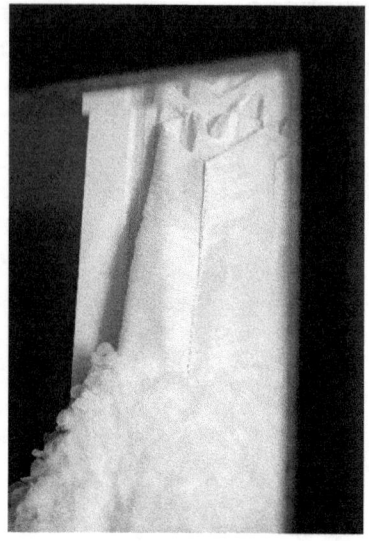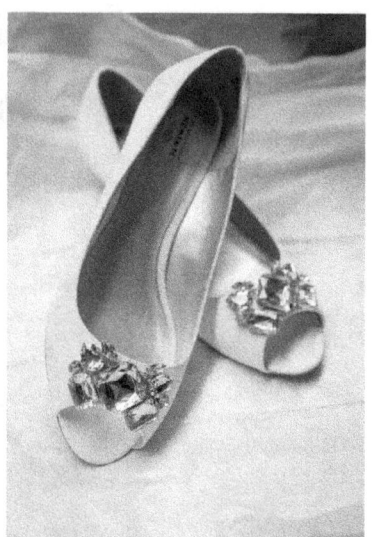

You could get shots like this with a borrowed dress, and a pair of sparkly shoes.

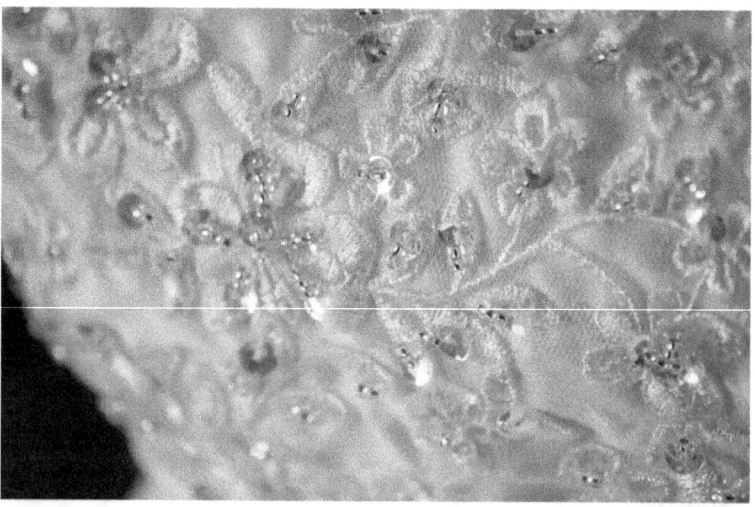

Make sure to take some close-up pictures of the details.

Chapter two

Skill Building

--In the Details—

In this saturated market, what will make your images stand out from all the other photographers? Let's talk a bit about your skills with a camera in general.

You may have been a photographer for many years, and you already know all about composition and f-stops and the rule of thirds. You may have an eye for detail, and know how to keep cluttered backgrounds from ruining a shot.

I'll assume that since you're reading this book that you already understand the basics of photography. If you don't there are a lot of great resources out there! I do want to cover a few things here that will be helpful for weddings specifically.

Weddings are about people. The shots of the details are important, but make sure to incorporate people as much as you can. Remember that we're telling a story, not just documenting objects. So get the shot of the wedding dress hanging up in a doorway, or from a tree branch. Then include some shots of the flower girl gazing up at the gown, the bride reaching out to run a hand over the satiny material, or any other way you can creatively add the element of human interest.

Have the bride hold the jewelry box with the ring in her hands, get the earrings as she puts them on, the veil draped over her face with window light illuminating the tulle. Don't limit your detail shots to items arranged out on a table or bed! Have her lift her skirt to show her shoes, instead of leaving them on a chair. Look for all the ways to include people in your images.

Another tip for detail shots is to focus on the details! An image of the bouquet resting on a chair won't be as effective if the shot includes the whole room. (Unless it's supposed to be a room shot that happens to have flowers in it!)

For detail shots, get in tight and lower your f-stop enough to get a clear focus on the item while keeping the rest of the picture soft. This can depend a bit on personal style of course, but it's a good rule of thumb.

I like to shoot details anywhere from f/1.4 to 4.0. You can use a macro lens to get in close for jewelry shots, or try some inexpensive macro filters that screw onto the lens you already have. Look on Amazon.com for the Vivitar Close-Up Macro Filter Set, and make sure you get the size that fits the diameter of your lens. These sets are well under $20, and are really fun to experiment with.

Did you know you can take whatever lens you have on your camera, remove it and flip it around so the wrong end is against your camera body, and it works as a macro lens? You can even buy adapters that allow you to attach it this way so you don't have to hold it. This method takes some practice to get the focusing right (your automatic focus won't work here!) but it's a lot of fun.

Another good idea is to put on a long lens (remember that off-brand 70-300mm lens I had in the beginning?) get WAY back, and zoom in for some fun detail shots. Zooming in instead of shooting from up close will compress the background and give the image a completely different look. You need a very steady hand, or better yet use a tripod or a solid surface to rest your camera on.

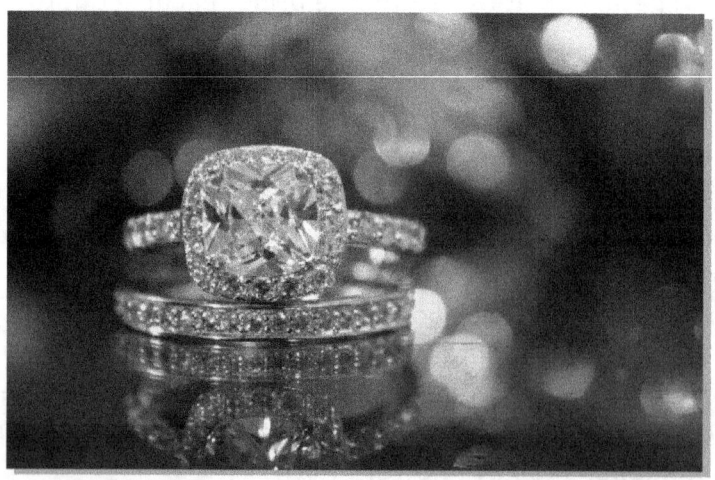

When you shoot details on a wedding day, it's a good idea to look around and find unique ways to showcase the items. Take some time to look at these types of images on Pinterest, to get inspiration.

I like to incorporate the theme of the wedding in the detail images. For example, at an outdoor wedding in a beautiful garden, I placed the bride's ring over the cone of a Black Eyed Susan blossom.

For simple elegance, look for a reflective surface to set the rings on. I always tuck an electronic tablet in my camera bag, so in a pinch I can set the rings on the black shiny surface of the screen!

Dental wax is another trade secret. It's that stuff the orthodontist gives to kids with braces, to apply to any wires that might poke out. This can be found online, and a small amount will hold a ring upright in defiance of gravity for those tricky shots.

--Let There Be Light--

That gives you some basics when it comes to detail photos, so let's talk about lighting. I love using natural light as much as possible! I love the natural, more organic feel I get when using window light or open shade outdoors.

Using natural light is NOT being lazy! You must know how to best use the light that is available in many different settings. When you have an off-camera flash, you are in control of the light. (Using OCF is a wonderful skill, and takes a lot of practice! I think every wedding photographer should have at least one Speedlight and know how to use it well if the need arises.)

I once had a well-meaning guest follow me around while I did pictures of the bridal party. He kept offering advice on my work, telling me that instead of having the group stand in the shade, I should put them in full sun while I stood in the shade.

I could probably write another book on lighting alone, but I'll just say that this is bad advice! I'm sure most of you know this already, but you want to look for open shade for your subjects. Make sure there's no dappled light filtering through the leaves, or slanting through gaps in a fence. You want to avoid those bright "hot spots" across faces. There's a lot that can be done to photos in post processing, but getting rid of those spots can be a nightmare!

Learn how to use reflectors. Your assistant can hold one, or you can have the group stand near the forward edge of the shadow so the brightly lit ground acts as a natural reflector. You want to have light bouncing back up into their faces, to keep their eyes from looking like dark raccoons.

Using natural light is something else that's easy to practice at home. You should feel confident about your abilities to shoot a properly exposed image in many types of light.

Whether you decide to concentrate on using natural light, or become proficient with off-camera flash, get lots of practice.

Keep an eye on any horizontal or vertical lines in your image as well. There's nothing professional about a website full of photos that are all crooked! Cameras are heavy, most of us have a weaker arm and it's easy to end up with a tilted image. But make sure to straighten all the pictures before you deliver the gallery.

Use a reference line that you know is straight, like the side of a building, the horizon, a chair leg, anything that's level. Use that line to adjust the image accordingly.

There is also lens distortion sometimes, which can make lines near the edges of the picture look off-level. In cases like this, I make sure the lines in the center of the picture are level.

I want to talk a little about cropping as well. It's easy to think "Oh, I'll just get the shot and crop it later."

But what happens when you take an image and crop out a third of it to get what you want? You lose pixels, your image shrinks, and if you want to print it in a large size you'll lose quality.

Get in the habit of cropping in-camera. Eliminate whatever you don't want by moving to one side or another, getting closer, zooming in or out, and checking your background for distractions. I rarely crop anything in post processing since I've gotten used to doing this.

It's also a good idea to pay attention to your background at all times. I once did an engagement session in a wooded area, so there were a lot of trees behind the couple. I was careful to check the space behind them while I shot, to make sure no tree trunks were aligned with their heads. (There's nothing pretty about a tree trunk "growing" out of someone's head!)

But in spite of my best efforts, there was a tree with rather thin branches that stuck out straight on either side, and I ended up giving the groom "antlers"!

In situations like this, it can help to shoot with a wider aperture (f/4 or lower) to help blur the background.

Watch for distractions before you press the shutter indoors as well. It's always easier to pause and move a wastebasket or folding chair in the background than to have to go through every image and try to clone over them or crop them out.

--Camera Setting Basics--

Now let's talk about camera settings. If you've been using the "P" mode, it's time to make a change! ("P" does not stand for professional!)

If you're already using another shooting mode, that's great! If not, making the switch to manual mode can be intimidating at first. But try using aperture priority (usually AV on your camera) to become more familiar with controlling your settings.

Shooting in AV mode allows you to select your aperture, (f-stop) and the camera figures out the proper shutter speed to match. This is the setting I use a great deal of the time, as I've found it's perfect for most situations I'm shooting in. I don't often need to manually adjust my shutter speed, but I can switch modes quickly if the need arises.

Shooting in aperture priority rather than program mode gives you more control over your images. You can quickly adjust your exposure compensation as well. So if you've been afraid to turn that dial away from "P", do it now!

If this is all new to you, find a good resource for beginning DSLR photography, and learn that first. Creativelive.com has some excellent classes for learning how to use a camera.

Another skill you'll need as a wedding photographer is post processing, also known as editing or "retouching" when mentioned to a client. This is where we talk about shooting in RAW versus JPEG.

If you're not already, set your camera to shoot in RAW format. This allows you to save images in post processing that otherwise would have been lost.

Basically, in RAW your camera saves all the data that it takes in when you press the shutter, so it's waiting there to be brought out if you need it. JPEG images have all that extra information deleted, the camera processes the image, and gives you the finished product. If it over- or under-exposed, you're pretty much out of luck. That area that looks black won't have any detail show up when you try to lighten it later.

Yes, shooing in RAW takes up more room on your memory card, but it will be worth it in the long run. Yes, you'll have to process the images in Lightroom and/or Photoshop, but those are skills you'll need to learn anyway!

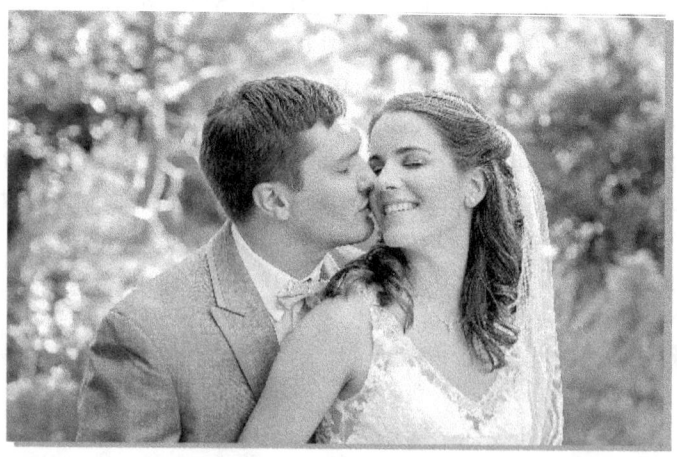

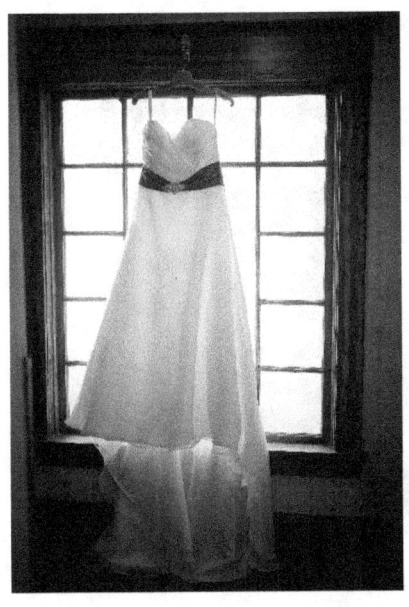

Here's a tip: bring a Command Hook in a pretty silver or white to hang a gown anywhere! They remove easily, and let you make the most of any situation. I used one here above this window.

The bride at one wedding brought these shoes for me to photograph, even though she wasn't going to wear them. They're the shoes she was wearing when her fiancé proposed! The boutonniere looks great when photographed on the groom's jacket.

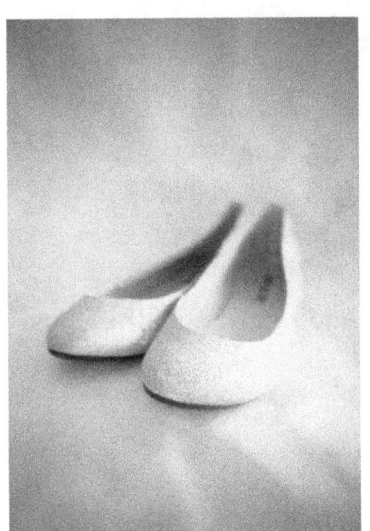

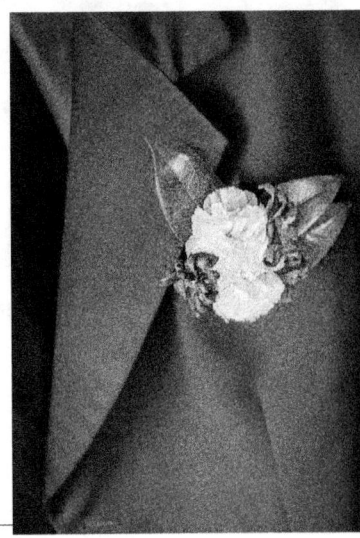

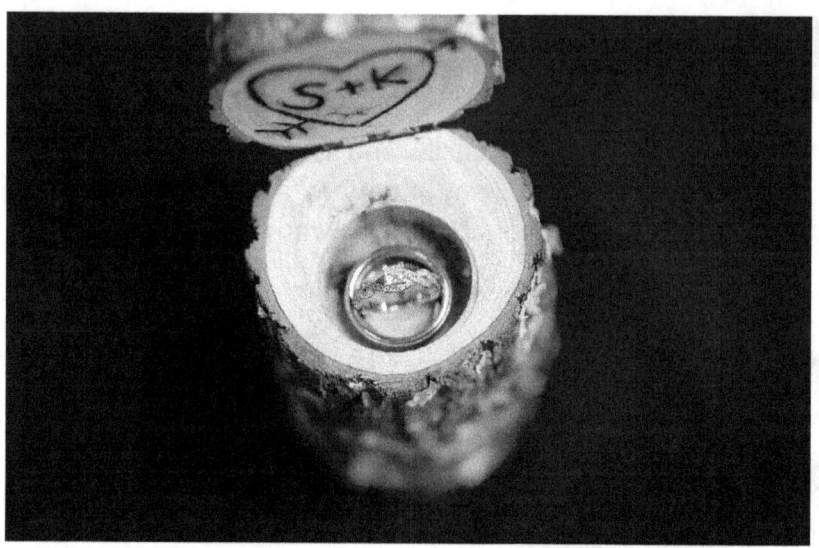

This bride and groom had a special ring holder with their initials wood-burned inside the lid.

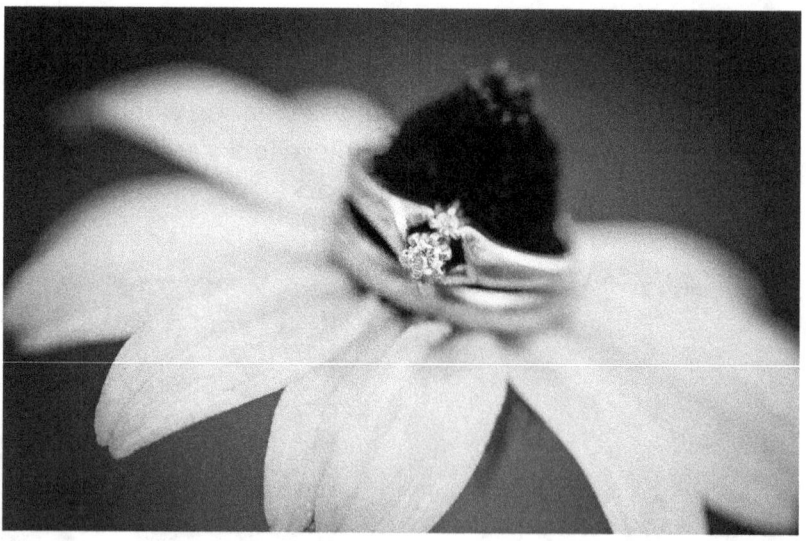

Look for flowers at outdoor weddings to hold the rings, and fit the theme of the day.

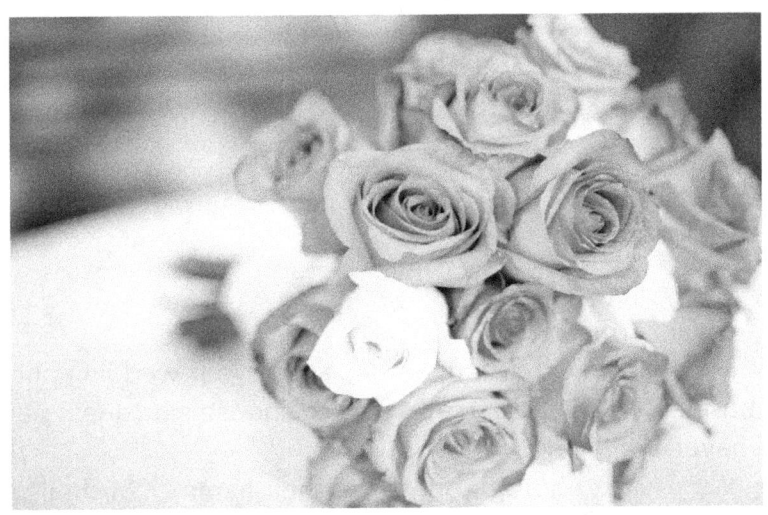

Make sure to get pictures of the bride's bouquet on its own.

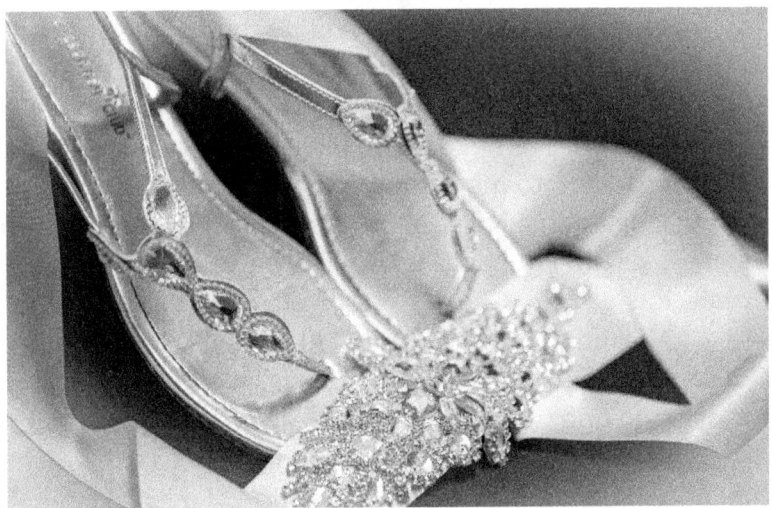

Here I grouped the shoes and sash together for an elegant arrangement.

Chapter Three

Starting Your Business

--Legal Formalities-

Now we're ready to talk about your wedding photography business! Of course you'll need to choose a business name, and maybe you already have.

Most photographers use their names: "Michelle Jones Photography". This sounds professional, and makes it easier for your clients when they don't have to remember two different names for you and your business.

However, if you have a name that's unusual or difficult to pronounce, you may want to choose something else. I hated the way my full name sounded as a business name: Rachel Raburn Photography. I've never liked having my first and last names both start with an R, to me it sounds like I'm chewing on something while I'm talking, with all the "Rrrrr" sounds. I know, that probably sounds silly to you, but I wanted to have a business name that I really loved.

I liked the idea of using "silver leaf", since it evokes an image of something shiny, elegant and expensive. I decided to combine those into one word, and created Silverleaf Photography.

For my glamour portraits, I decided to use my first and middle names, which is another option. So I also have Rachel Nicole Photography, of Silverleaf Studios.

If you have two very distinct genres of photography that you shoot, I think it's a good idea to use separate names. Keep them separate on your website as well.

Whatever name you chose, you'll need to register your business name and get a tax ID number from the IRS. You can register your business online at **http://irs-tax-id.com**.

You'll need to select the type of business you want to set up, the two main choices being Sole Proprietor/Individual and Limited Liability Company (LLC). If you are married with assets, it could be a better choice to go with an LLC. This protects your personal assets in case of a lawsuit.

Next, find out if your county requires photographers to be licensed, by contacting your Chamber of Commerce. If so, this usually costs $50.

Once you have a business name, tax ID and license, talk to your insurance agent about liability coverage. You may never need it, but it makes your clients feel better knowing you have it! You should insure your gear against theft and damage as well. It may already be covered by your renter's or homeowner's policy, but ask to make sure.

You also need to come up with a contract for your clients to sign. I'm including a sample contract in the final chapter, but it's a good idea to go over your contract with a lawyer to make sure it covers the specific laws in your area.

It's also a good idea to have the bride and groom sign a model release form, if this isn't included in your contract. If you ever want to use pictures of them for advertising, you'll need to have this! You can find an example in the last chapter.

--Money Matters--

Now comes the fun part: figuring out how much to charge! Deciding on your prices can be one of the most difficult aspects of starting your business!

When you first get started, you'll charge much less than you will down the road. People are taking a risk in hiring you, and they won't want to pay top dollar for someone with very little experience. But don't make the mistake of working for free! You should charge something for what you do, even if it's just a token amount. You should work for clients who value photography, not someone who's looking for the cheapest photographer they can find.

I shot my first wedding for $250, and ended up with $300 in expenses. That included camera and lens rental, gas, advertising that got me the job, black slacks and comfortable shoes. I didn't realize it would cost so much, but I figured losing $50 wasn't too bad for my first try!

Before you set prices, you need to figure out your expenses. There are probably more of them than you realize! Here is my own expense list from the first six months of my business:

- Website $120
- Equipment purchases $234
- Equipment rentals $720
- Gas $220
- Clothing $125
- Camera Bag (used) $15
- Sample canvas print and album $240
- Client albums $400
- Blank CDs and jewel cases $45
- Photoshop ($10 per month) $60
- Animoto.com (slideshow creator) $140
- Photoshop templates $55
- Actions and presets $200
- Advertising with Google AdWords $100
- Advertising on Thumbtack.com $131
- Babysitter $160

I'm sure there was a little more that I didn't keep track of, but this was most of it. That's a grand total of $2,960 in business expenses for six months. That comes out to $493 per month.

I shot seven weddings during that time, so that's $422 per wedding in expenses.

Now let's look at how much money I actually brought in. The amount I was paid (They varied from $150 to $700 per wedding) averages out to $420 each. Can you see the problem here? Not only did I fail to earn a profit or get paid for my time, I actually lost money!

It *cost* me money to shoot seven weddings over six months. And I gave away hundreds of hours of my time for free! I did gain a great deal of experience, and loved what I was doing. So I looked at it as having my expenses covered for my favorite hobby!

I realized that I needed to raise my prices however, if I wanted to make this "hobby" into a business that I could profit from.

So here's what you need to do: figure out your expenses as well as you can, then decide how much you want to earn per hour. The typical wedding will be 4-8 hours of shooting time on the actual day, and you can add another two or three hours if you meet your clients for a consultation and engagement session. Editing your photos will take you 3-4 hours per hour of shooting. That means you'll spend anywhere from 20-40 hours of your time on each wedding.

If you want to earn $15 per hour, you'll need to figure on $300-$600 for your time. Then add that to your expenses per wedding.

During that first six months, my prices barely covered my expenses, and I didn't earn a dime for my time. You *can't* charge $300 for a wedding and still make money, no matter how hard it may be for some of your early clients to understand.

Now, I'd like to make more than $15 per hour. I'm a wife and homeschooling mother of five, and my time is precious to me! To make it worth the hassle and the time away from family, I'd rather start my rates at $50 per hour.

I've also had more experience, and gained artistic skills that make me more valuable than I was when I first started.

If I start with a $50 per hour rate for an average wedding, that's $2,000 before expenses. And $2,000 is about average for where I live. Here in Central Oregon the going rate is between $1,500 and $4,500. I'm sure there are many above and below that range, but the majority are in that ballpark.

I do want to keep my prices within reach of most brides, so my basic package is $3,200. Since I've changed my collections over the last year to include higher-end products, my costs have gone up. So I now assume a base cost of $750 per wedding. This includes business expenses and cost of goods. I add $100 for my equipment replacement fund, my second shooter's fee ($200), travel costs, and the $2,000 for my time.

Add that all together and you get $3,150. That doesn't include the engagement session, which I include for free. So you can see that my lowest priced collection is perfectly calculated for me, and the way I run my business.

I have some wiggle room if a bride is on a tight budget, but as soon as I lower my price my income-per-hour starts dropping. I don't want to work for less than $30 per hour (which gives me $800 total to offer in discounts) and that's my minimum. Decide where you'll draw the line and stick to it!

You may be able to charge just a few hundred dollars when you're first getting started, if you don't mind giving away your time to gain experience and build your portfolio. Just keep in mind that you won't make any real profit as long as you do this.

So many photographers out there lack the confidence to charge what they're worth! Don't feel bad about charging enough to make a living. If you truly have the skill and personality to do an amazing job, you'll find clients who will gladly pay you for your service.

Of course, as the years go by you'll need to raise your prices a bit each year. You'll be more skilled and will have further developed your gift of artistic vision. You may have won a contest or two, and had images published on nationally known wedding blogs or magazines. You'll be worth more by virtue of your growing value as an artist.

--In Need of Assistants--

I want to mention here that not every photographer uses a second shooter. Some of the top wedding photographers work alone, and do an amazing job! But even they have assistants to help with multiple tasks beyond taking pictures.

Please, never shoot a wedding alone! I only shot one wedding by myself, and it was a pain in the neck – literally! Carrying the camera bag, both cameras and all my gear was exhausting. It was also difficult and time consuming to get everything myself when I needed it, instead of having someone standing by and waiting to hand it to me.

Even if you don't plan on having a second shooter, bring an assistant. I had family members help out for free early on, which was wonderful.

Obviously, when I first started out I couldn't afford to pay an assistant anyway! My husband came with me my first year, and we made a great team.

The only problem I had was people who didn't know us would come up to him to ask him things like "where do you want the bride and groom to stand for cutting the cake?"

I guess since he's a man, people assumed he was the head photographer! He would just smile, point at me and say "Ask her, she's the one in charge!"

Your assistant can carry gear and pass equipment when you need it, but you can also let them take pictures if you want. Before I started hiring a second shooter, I allowed my assistants to take whatever photos they wanted, as long as I didn't currently need the camera they were holding.

I gave basic pointers, and told them to focus on getting candid shots. It didn't matter if the assistant wasn't a pro, and I'd throw out 90% of what they were shooting. And you know what? The 10% that was useable was sometimes great!

I've been pleasantly surprised by the pictures my assistants have taken, and it's always worth sorting through them to find 2 or 3 unexpected gems.

Just make sure your assistant signs a release form, giving you and your business all rights to the pictures they take. They're taking pictures while working for you, and they have to understand that you will be using them with no strings attached. I'll put a contract for second shooters in the last chapter.

We've now covered the legal issues and pricing strategies. Next you need to set up a website.

--Your Website and Advertising—

There are so many great companies out there to help you start your own website, it's gotten easier than ever for people like us.

I decided to use Zenfolio.com for mine, since they have so many great templates and it's very user-friendly. I have the deluxe version, which means I can purchase my own domain name through somewhere like GoDaddy.com or Web.com, and have it point to my Zenfolio.com site.

That means instead of my clients typing in **www.silverleafphotography.zenfolio.com**, they can simply use **www.SilverleafPhoto.com**. This makes it look more professional.

Here's a referral code that will save you 10% off a new Zenfolio account: A8R-CZ3-N6R. You can also put my user name (silverleafphotography) as a referral code. (Disclaimer: yes, this gives me a few dollars credit to my account, while saving you money at the same time!)

Make sure your website is simple and easy to navigate. Put your best images on your home page to grab the viewer and draw them in. You want them to stay and keep looking, and they won't do that if your website is complicated or appears unprofessional.

You should put your name and phone number where it's clearly visible on your home page as well, and make it easy for potential clients to contact you.

Make sure to keep your contact information updated if you move or change you cell phone number.

Now you can sit back and wait for your phone to start ringing, and all those clients to come pouring in! And wait... and wait.... Where are they? Oh that's right, you haven't advertised!

Advertising can become a huge expense, very quickly. For someone just starting out, especially if you don't have a lot of cash to invest in your business, this can drain all your reserves in a hurry.

Plus, you're probably trying to find some lower-paying jobs, just to get your foot in the door. It hardly seems sensible to spend $300 on advertising to book one $400 wedding client. So what do you do?

I tried Google AdWords for a few months, which I liked since they allow you to set a budget. You can decide how much you want to spend each month, and it won't go over that.

I also got a coupon for $75 off my first $100, so it only cost me $25! I figured it was worth a shot for that price.

I tracked how many clicks my ad was getting, leading clients to my website. There were a lot more than I expected, which was a pleasant surprise. Unfortunately, none of those clicks led to any inquiries. Nobody contacted me, and I didn't get any work from that ad.

You might have more success than I did, and it may be worth a try especially if you find a similar discount.

Many photographers use Facebook ads for marketing with huge success. It's worth a try, and with the ability to target a specific audience, it will help get your business in front of your ideal client.

My next approach was Thumbtack.com. I don't even remember where I heard about this website, but I loved it! The way it works is simple: you create a profile for free, with your contact information, some sample photos and a Q&A page for potential clients.

You set up what kind of jobs you're wanting to find (weddings, family, seniors, etc...) and set what price ranges you have in mind.

Then the beauty of the system kicks in! People looking for photographers will fill out a questionnaire on the website, and describe their work request. If it matches the type of client you're looking for, Thumbtack sends you an email with the information. You can review the request, see what the details are and what their budget is, and decide if you want to send a quote.

That's where you actually pay for the service. Each quote you send will require a certain number of credits, which you can buy ahead of time or per-credit as you need them. The average wedding requires anywhere from $15-$25 to send a quote, depending on the budget the client has set. (The higher-paying the job, the more it costs to send a quote.)

As I shared earlier in my expense report from the first six months, I spent a total of $131 sending quotes on Thumbtack.com. This wasn't just for weddings, but I also sent quotes for senior portraits, family sessions and a few others. (Those are considerably cheaper to send quotes on than weddings.)

I ended up getting all seven of those weddings I shot from Thumbtack. I also got one senior session, and one family portrait session, as well as a 50th anniversary party! That works out to about $13 in quotes to get each job.

It's a great way to get your business seen by people who are looking for a photographer, and like I did, you might even find a few smaller jobs to help fill in your schedule.

Actually, I found that those short photo sessions were far more profitable than the first six months of weddings! I charged $150 for a 45-minute session, and that included 30-40 digital images on CD.

I figured that each session took about an hour with travel time, and another 2 hours editing the photos afterwards. That's $50 an hour for my time, and almost no costs involved!

And how much was I making shooting weddings during that same time frame? Well, nothing.

So don't hesitate to advertise in areas other than weddings. It will help spread awareness of your business, build your portfolio, and in the first few months to a year of your business it may be your biggest source of income!

I don't use Thumbtack anymore, since most of the clients who look for quotes there are budget shoppers, looking for a cheap photographer. But when you're just getting started, it's a great resource!

I mentioned targeting your ideal client with advertising. Before you can do that, you need to figure out who your ideal client is! Sit down and figure this out right now. Are they college-educated, upper class, dog-loving and fashionable? Hikers, nature-enthusiasts, natural food-eating free spirits? What magazines do they buy? What books and movies do they love? What kind of music do they listen to? Deciding the answers to these questions will help you target your ads to find the clients you want.

It will also help you to refine your brand, which we'll get into very soon!

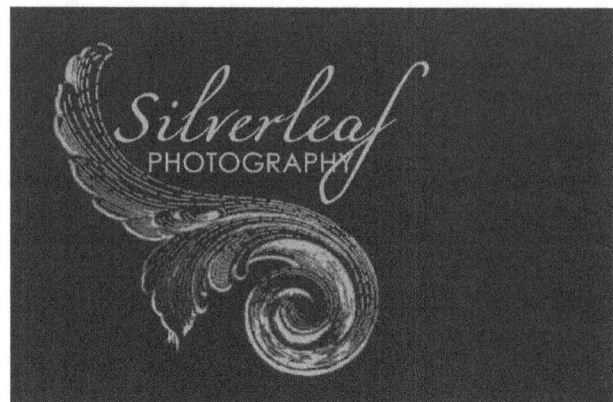 This was my first logo, that I designed myself. I knew I wanted something elegant and a little vintage. However, I decided that I didn't want to have so much black, and that it needed to be more light and soft.

This is the next one I designed, that I'm still using now. It's brighter and softer, but still has a touch of elegance with the chandelier and the metallic silver script.

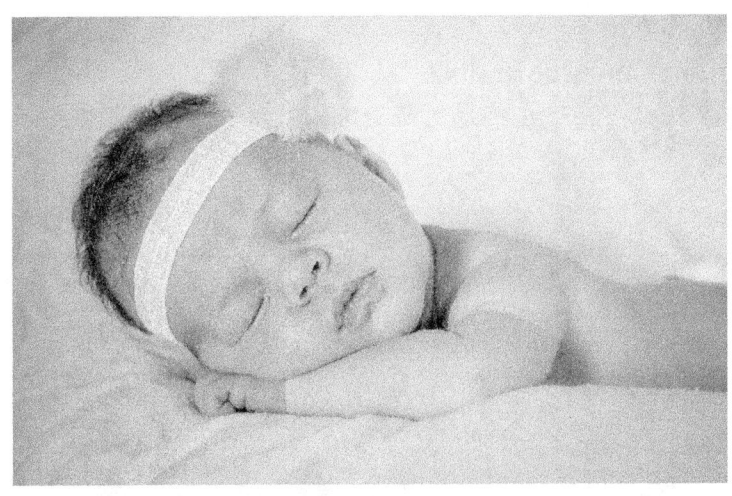

Here's an example of some other photography jobs I took in between weddings. I did newborns...

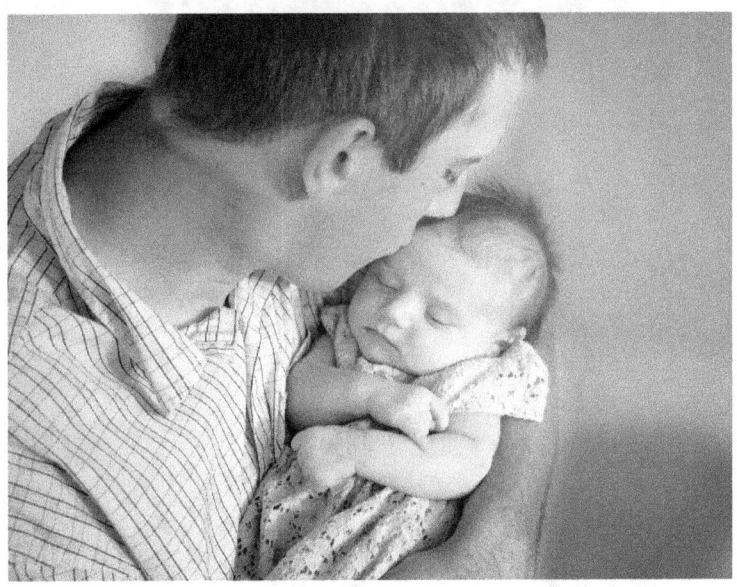

And family portraits...

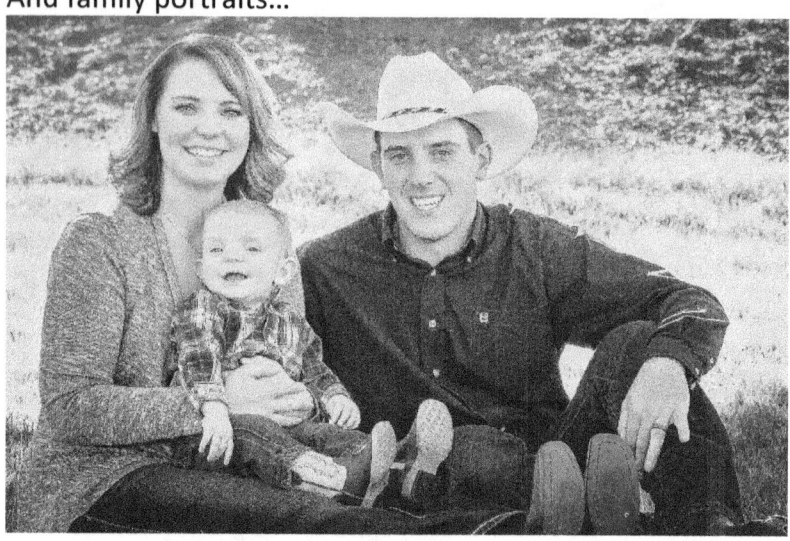

...And a Senior Session.

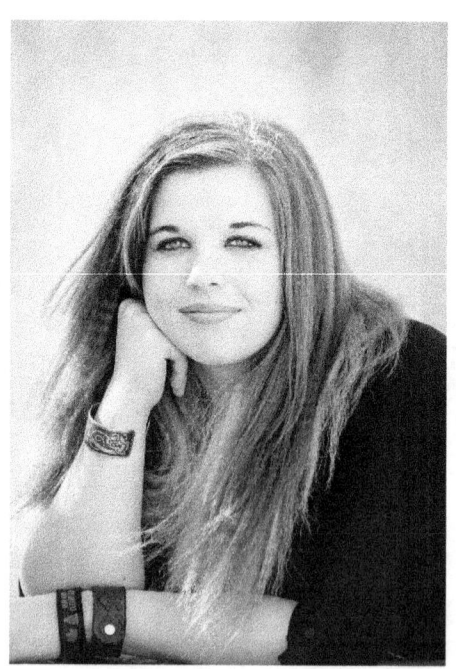

Chapter Four

Telling the Story

--How to Tell the Story—

This is supposed to be a book on story-telling with wedding photography, so let's get started on that! Honestly, it was learning about this approach to shooting weddings that gave me the incentive I needed to start my own business. It fits with my own style perfectly, and it's something a lot of clients want.

I'll go over the basic styles of wedding photography first, then describe what makes story-telling unique.

Traditional/Classic wedding photography can be described as posed, planned, structured, scheduled and predictable. The photos are of the main events and families lined up in rows smiling at the camera.

The polar opposite to the traditional method is the Photo-Journalistic approach. That's usually a collection of candid images, lots of details and emotions, and all the little unscripted moments from the day. The photographer is "invisible", not giving direction.

Illustrative photography is a method I use when doing engagement sessions. It places the focus on composition, background and lighting. Placing the couple in the chosen environment, then letting them relax and interact naturally.

Portraiture is technically precise, formal and posed. Fine Art Portraiture is similar, with an edgier European vibe.

Many photographers lean one way or the other, some combining aspects of various methods. One of those combinations is what I call Story-Telling photography.

Story telling means capturing the moments that tell the complete story of the wedding day. It combines the Photojournalistic 'in the background' candid shots with the Traditional family group and bridal party shots, as well as Portraiture and Illustrative techniques. Here's how it translates into an actual wedding shoot:

I'll arrive when the bride is getting her hair and makeup done, and include close-up shots of her shoes, jewelry, rings, flowers, veil and gown. I'll use creative composition and framing techniques to capture the bride getting her dress laced up, with any friends and family members who are there to help.

I may include the bride's reflection in a mirror, or the mother helping to adjust her sash. Maybe the flower girl will come running in to gaze up at the ladies with adoring eyes, or she'll crouch down to see the bride's sparkly shoes.

I won't forget the hugs, laughter, champagne, trays of snacks, and any decorations or themes that might be present. I try to capture all of the five senses that surround the bride.

So far this has been a very Photojournalistic approach. I want the bride to become comfortable with my presence, so I start off as unobtrusively as possible.

However, I don't just photograph everything as it is. I'll add in a dash of Illustrative photography, by helping to set up certain portions of the environment.

If the bride is getting her makeup done in a chair that's angled away from the best window light, or is too close to an overly bright window, I'll ask the make-up artist if we can shift things around for some pictures. I may ask her to re-create some moments that may have occurred before I arrived, like sweeping blush onto the bride's cheeks or spraying hairspray or touching up lipstick.

I want the images to be as natural as possible, with ideal lighting and a non-posed feel to them.

Once the bride is ready, if there's time, we'll get some pictures of the bride alone. These bridal portraits tend to be more posed, Portraiture type images. They're the ones that make every bride feel beautiful and glamorous, and set off her best features.

Then we'll pull in the other girls for some group shots. These tend to be more posed and Classic, with lots of fun and laughter added in. They'll probably have certain ideas for poses that they want to try, and I'll also snap candid moments of interaction in between.

All of these elements put together will tell the story of that pre-wedding hour, more than focusing on the bride alone. You're not eliminating all the traditional photos, just greatly enhancing and adding to them!

Meanwhile, my second shooter is taking similar pictures in the suite where the groom and his guys are getting ready. The shots to look for here are the buddies laughing and toasting with their drinks, helping each other with ties or cufflinks, putting on their shoes, the groom in a quiet moment of contemplation, maybe his reflection in a mirror or window, etc...

Once both 'teams' are ready, we'll meet up for the first look. Not every couple wants to see each other before the ceremony, but it's something I recommend to all my clients. Choose a great location ahead of time, clear everyone else out of the area, and have the groom wait there with his back turned.

The bride approaches, walks up to him and taps him on the shoulder. When he turns around and sees her there, it's magical.

My second shooter and I take up opposite positions for this, to capture both the bride's and groom's faces at the same time. (Just make sure to stay out of each other's shots!) We use a long lens, like a 70-200, so we can stay out of the couple's way and make it feel like a private moment.

This is similar to the Illustrative method. We set up the environment, and let the couple interact naturally.

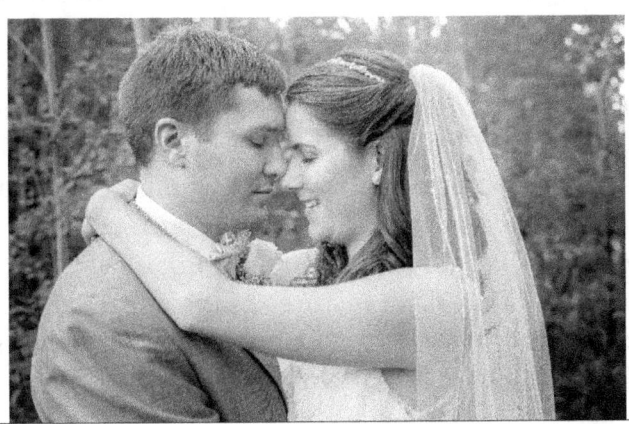

Once we cover the first look, we'll move right into the bride and groom couple's portraits. This transitions us again to Portraiture, for those "Romance novel cover" photos that will be stunning in the album and on large canvases.

If the first look took place somewhere other than the ceremony venue, I'll try to leave for the wedding venue ahead of the bridal party. This allows me to take pictures of the venue before the ceremony.

Again, I try to be creative (Photojournalistic) and get interesting detail shots that will hold special memories for the couple. This may include their program propped against a floral centerpiece, a shot from low to the ground of the candles or flowers lining the aisle, and any elements of the ceremony like a unity candle or colored sand.

I pay attention as the guests are arriving, and get photos of family members who haven't seen each other in years giving a tearful embrace. The happy anticipation of a wedding leads to lots of laughter and smiles, excited children and lovely memories.

I'll also take this time to figure out exactly where I'll position myself for the ceremony. It's extremely helpful to visit a venue before the wedding, and get a good idea of where the best places will be. But on the day of the wedding, things may unfold a bit differently than you'd thought, and you'll need to find a good alternative quickly!

Also, I find the officiant when I arrive at the venue and introduce myself if we haven't met. I'll ask if he has any restrictions on where I can stand.

As the ceremony begins, that's when having a second shooter becomes really helpful! I position myself at the head of the aisle, usually crouching just next to the first row of chairs. From this position I can take pictures of the groom when the bride appears, and quickly swivel to get the bride and her father.

My second will stay at the end of the aisle where the bride will be appearing. They'll get pictures of the guests as they all stand and turn to face the bride (that's a photo every bride *loves*!) as well as the bride from behind as she walks toward her smiling groom.

In addition to wide-angle shots, they'll use a longer lens to get pictures of the ceremony as it happens. That give us a blend of my down-and-in-front images with the from-the-back perspective of my second shooter.

I'll usually slip from one side of the aisle to the other at least once, to get an angle that shows both the bride and groom's faces.

I find that staying near the front eliminates the problem of guests getting in the way by holding their cameras or phones into the aisle. If the area is very small, and I can't stay in the front, I'll move back down the aisle slightly while staying down low.

I know photos taken from a low angle aren't always flattering, but I don't want to stand up in the middle of the ceremony taking pictures! Of course, if the audience is all standing (right at the beginning, or later on for prayer if it's a religious service) I'll stand as well.

From my lower vantage point I'll focus on the couple's faces, their hands as they exchange rings, and of course the kiss! I do stand up for that sometimes, since nobody will be looking at me anyway.

I know my second shooter is in the back, getting shots from a better angle. So that combination works really well for us. They're also in a great position for pictures of the newly married couple as they walk back up the aisle.

Occasionally the couple will opt to skip the first look, so we'll take some time immediately after the ceremony and go outside (weather permitting) for the bride and groom portraits.

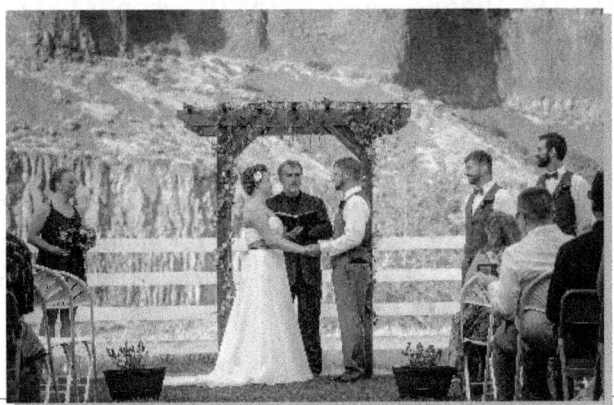

While I'm working, I always keep the story in mind. I'm also shooting for the album that I'll create later, and I want each page to tell a special part of the story. One thing that's important are moments that show the beginning of a new "chapter" in the story. It may be the bride getting out of the limo, the bridal party walking up steps into to venue, or the bride and groom leaving the ceremony hand in hand.

These pictures show movement from one place to another, and help transition the reader (the person viewing the album) from one part of the story to the next.

I also keep the album in mind while shooting the couple's portraits. I make sure to get some amazing wide angle shots that include the landscape, for an impressive two-page album spread.

At this point (usually during cocktail hour) you'll have to go through the chaos of family pictures. It helps to find a family member or guest who knows everyone, and have them help gather the necessary people for each group.

I try to keep this Traditional session as up-beat as possible, by telling little jokes or saying things like "Come on, try to look like you like each other!" That usually lightens the mood.

My second will stand behind me and off to one side, taking candid shots while I focus on getting everyone to look at me. I make sure to tell them to ignore my assistant, so I don't have people looking in two directions.

I'll ask other guests gathered around me with their own cameras and phones to wait and let me get the shot, then I'll lower my camera and let them snap away for 10 seconds. Making this known in a simple and polite manner ahead of time usually keeps everyone happy!

If the ceremony and reception are at the same location, we'll get shots of the reception before any guests arrive. Usually the bride and groom disappear for a few minutes following the ceremony, and they may be standing in a receiving line for a while after that. That's a good time to get pictures of the reception area before we start the family portraits.

Now the reception is beginning. We already took pictures of the details (table decorations, flowers, the cake and/or cupcakes, personalized napkins and wine glasses) before the guests came in, so now we focus on other details.

I'll get some attractive food shots, maybe the row of wine bottles at the bar, and any custom drinks, or a server carving a roast. Before everyone starts eating, we'll try to get pictures that include every guest. It's pretty easy to walk up to a group of four of five people who are chatting and holding drinks, say "hi, could I get your picture?" They'll all lean together and smile, then 'click' and we're on to the next group.

Most people don't like to have their picture taken while they're eating, so we try to stay out of the way during dinner. This is the time when we try to eat a quick meal. I always ask the bride well in advance if there will be a meal for myself and my second shooter, and they've always provided for us. But just in case, we bring a granola bar!

I make sure to ask the bride ahead of time, because it's important that we are able to eat at the same time as the bridal party and not after all the guests have been served.

Here's why: I once shot a wedding where we had to wait and go through the buffet after almost all the guests had gone through. My second shooter and I sat down in a small unused room off the back, and had barely gotten two bites down when we heard the DJ announce "All right everyone, it's time for the toasts!"

We looked at each other in disbelief, jumped up and ran like crazy to the other side of the building where we'd stashed our camera gear, and dashed back to the reception hall just in time!

So (back to the timeline!) once we have our food we sit down and eat. This may be the only few minutes of sitting down that we get all day. So we enjoy it, drink a bottle of water, and get ready to keep going.

We'll make sure to capture the toasts, getting the reactions of the bride and groom and other guests. Some fun shots of the bride looking at the groom and laughing at the best man's jokes, of the groom leaning over to kiss his new wife.

Don't forget, we're telling a story! Watch for emotions, reactions, hugs, laughter, and turn around to capture the guests lifting their champagne glasses to toast the couple.

When the dancing starts, we'll be in place to capture the first dance. Dance photos are so much fun, I love the pictures of Grandma and Grandpa slow dancing, the flower girl pulling the ring bearer (who's dying of embarrassment) around the dance floor, and the bride's maids rocking out to their favorite song.

There is usually a special father-daughter dance, mother-son dance, and the newlywed couple take to the floor with a special song. My second shooter and I will take different sides of the room, not opposite each other but one on each side of an "L" shape. That gives us a better chance of catching special moments if one of us gets blocked by another guest.

We'll use off-camera flash as needed, and also crank up our ISO and get some without flash if it's not too dark.

After the Photojournalistic approach to the toasts and dancing, we change to Illustrative for the cake cutting. We'll show the couple the best place to stand, make sure they know how to hold the knife and the basics of how to do the cake cutting, then we stand back and take pictures while they have fun.

Same thing goes for the bouquet and garter toss: we set up the area, plan the angle and where we want to stand, then let the event unfold.

The evening comes to a close with the couple leaving through a cascade of rice, or a shower of petals, or a blaze of sparklers or a fairytale of bubbles. They drive away and the party is over, and we are done at last!

We switched seamlessly from Photojournalism to Traditional, to Portraiture, to Illustrative, and all over the map again and again! This hybrid of styles is the perfect way to tell any couple's wedding story.

The following images will help to give examples of the timeline I explained above.

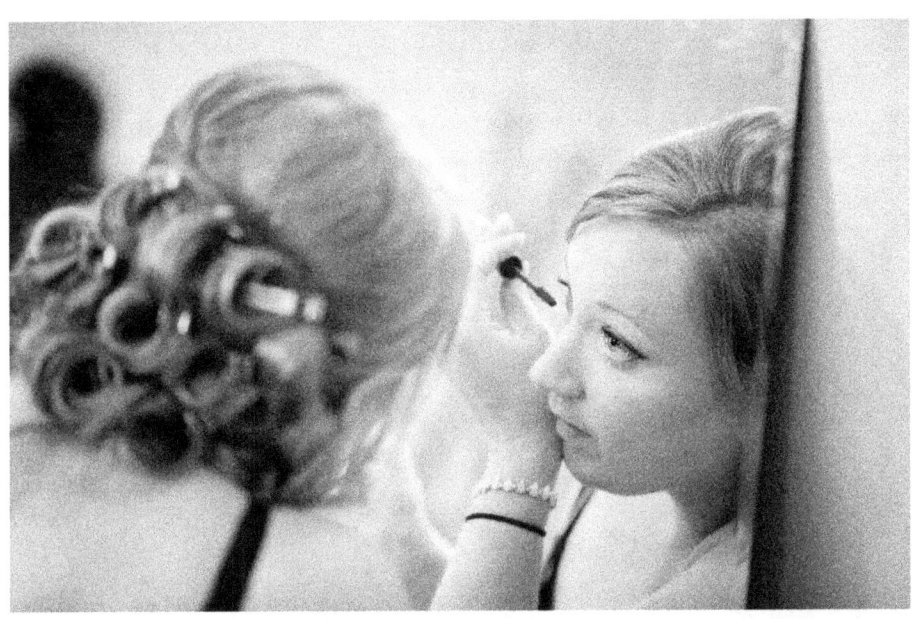

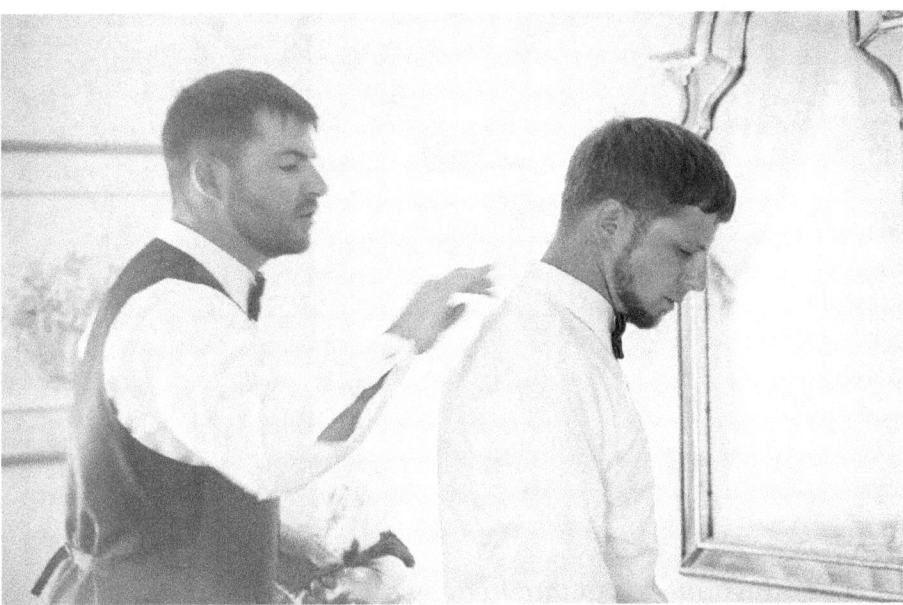

Getting ready: the bride touches up her makeup and the best man helps the groom.

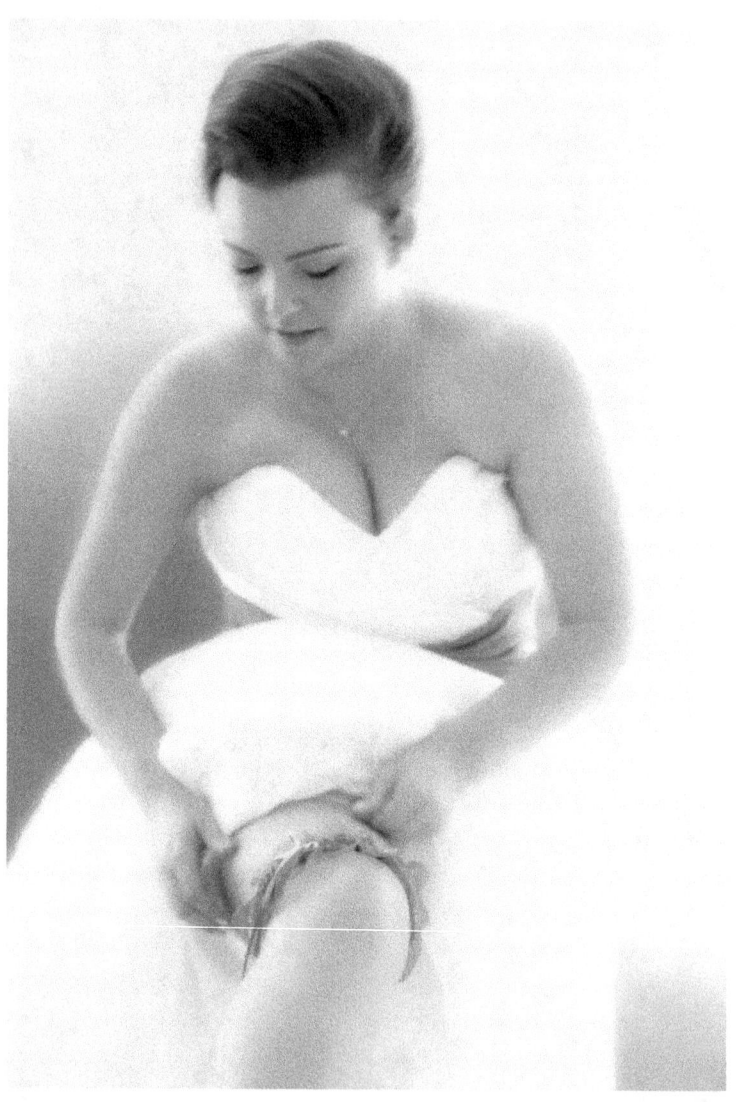

Time for the bride to get into her gown! Don't forget the special
moments while the bride is getting ready, like putting on her garter,
and any jewelry she's wearing.

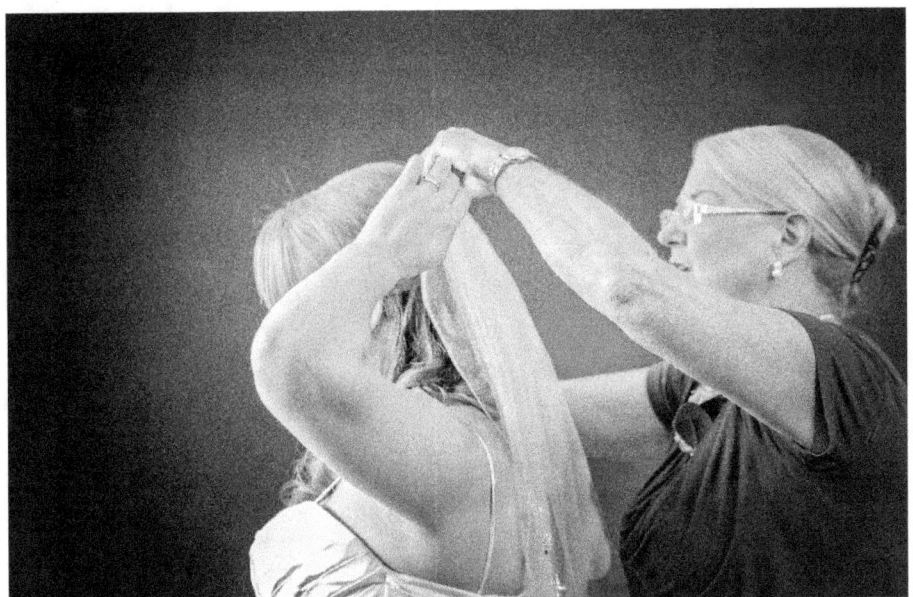

I always try to include images of the bride's mother or close friends helping her dress.

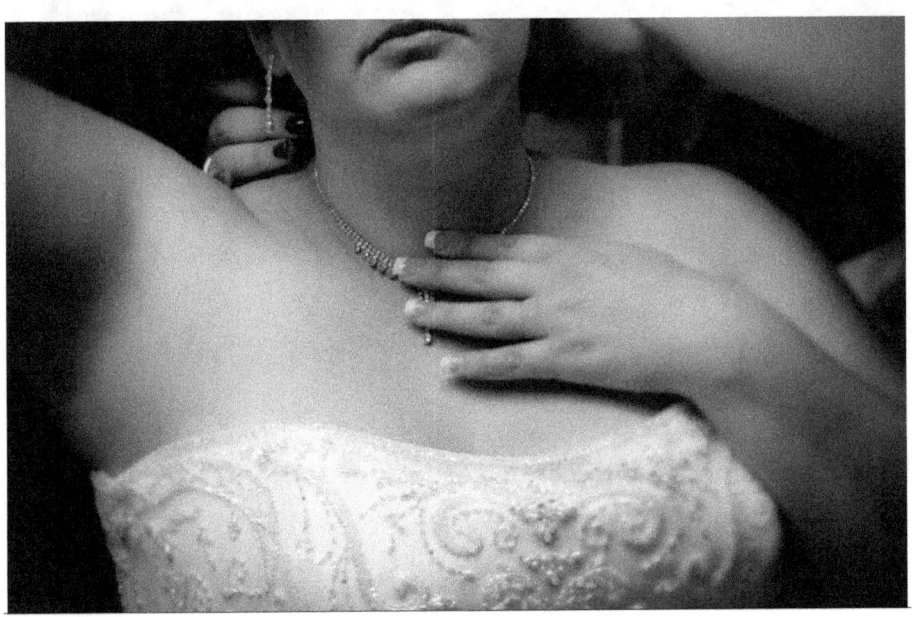

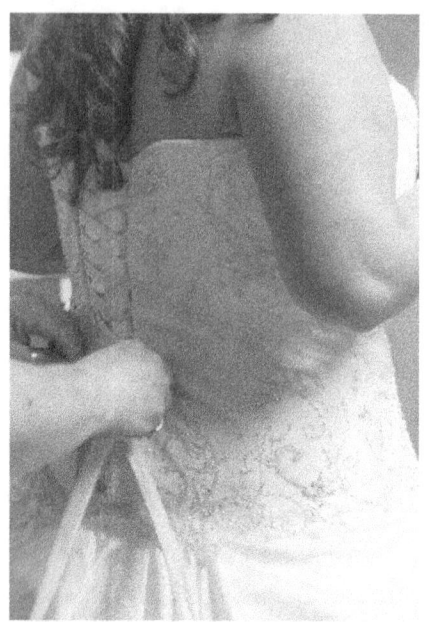
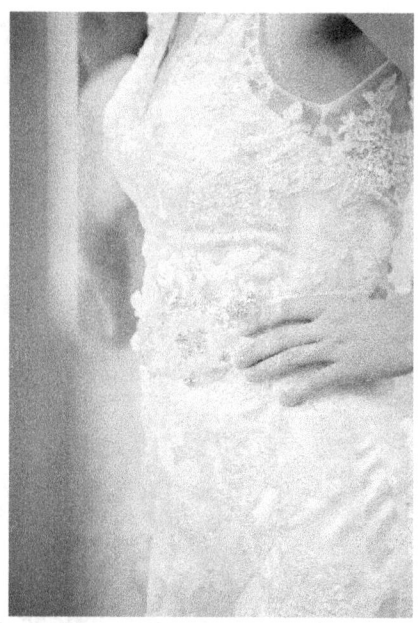
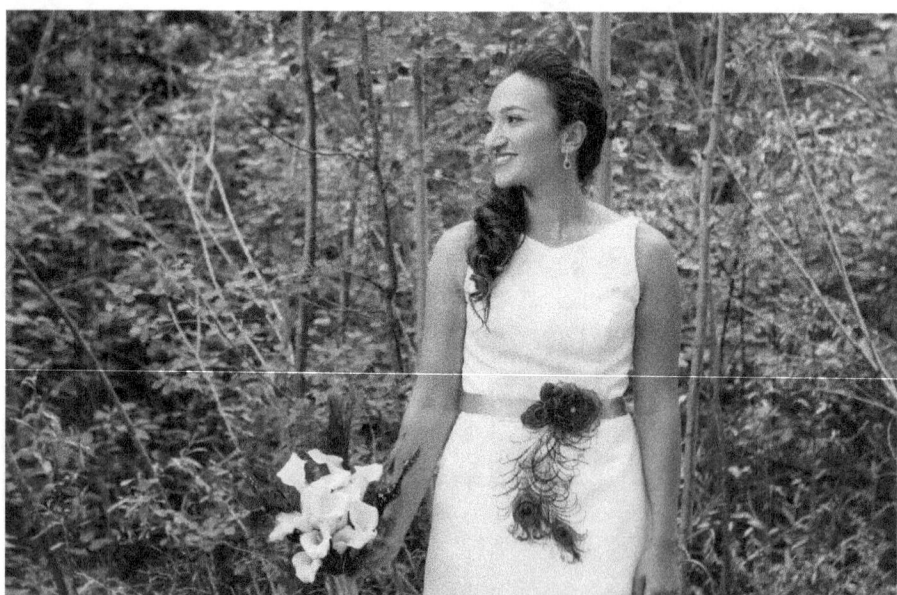

The final moments of the bride getting dressed, and we're just minutes away from the first look!

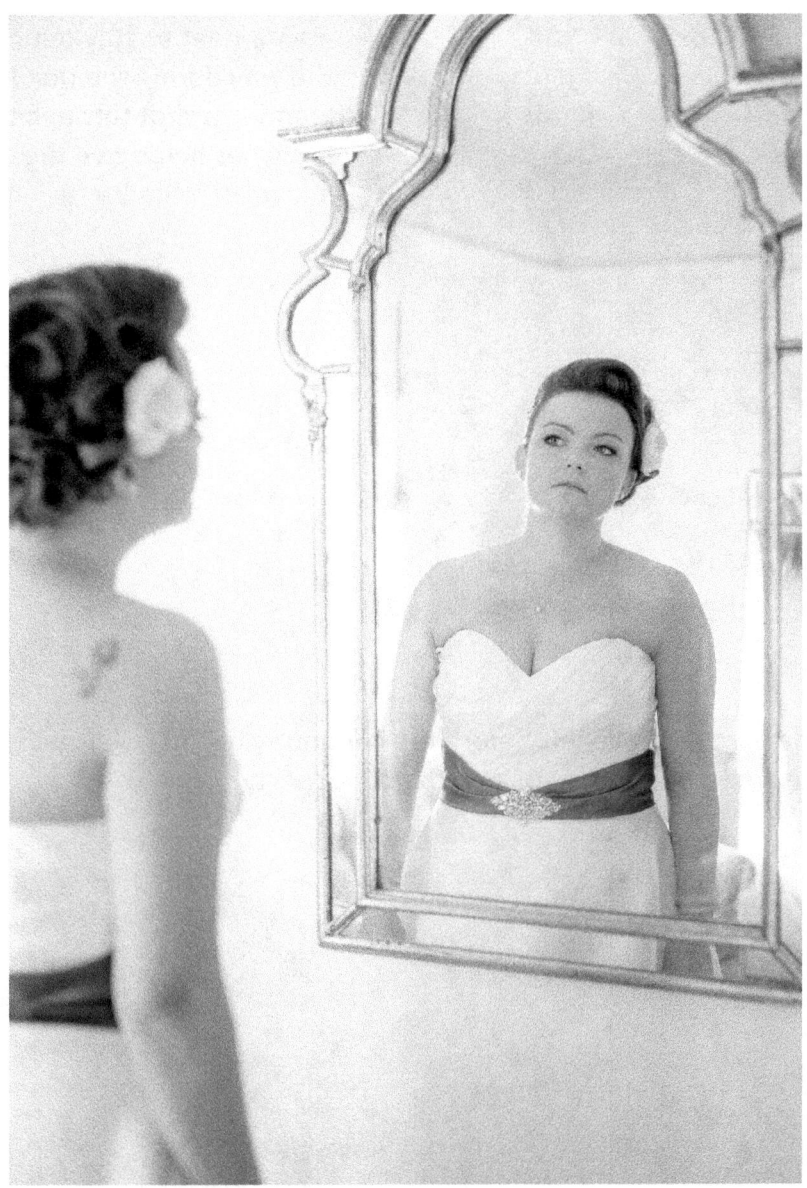

When I found this gorgeous mirror at this venue, I was thrilled! Once the bride was ready, I brought her into this location to make sure all the details of her wardrobe were in place. Notice how the curves of the mirror echo the shape of her head and shoulders?

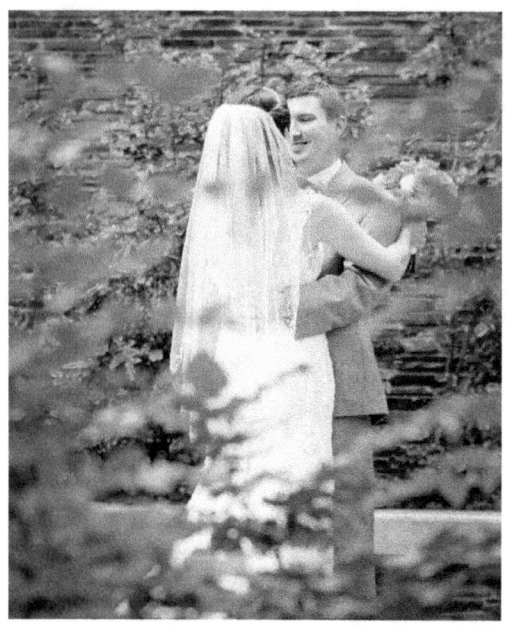

Remember to stay out of the way during the first look. Framing a shot through tree branches helps give the image an intimate feeling.

In the time we have left before the ceremony begins, we'll get the bride and groom portraits and the bridal party.

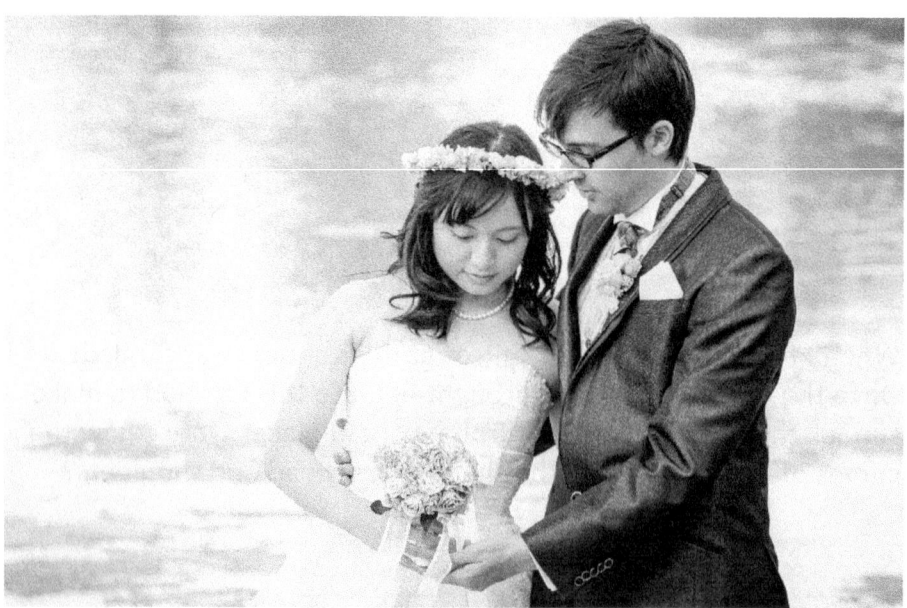

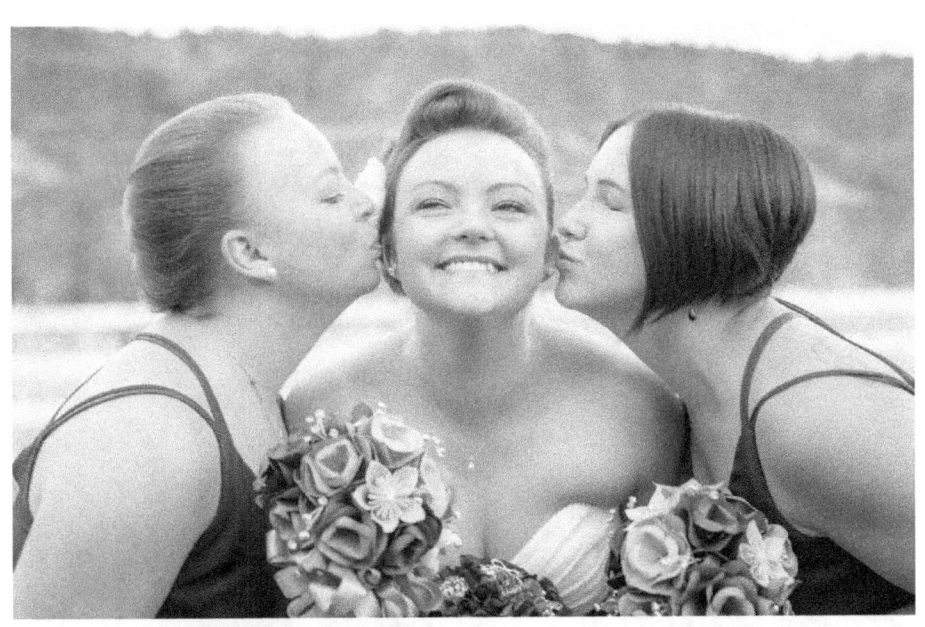

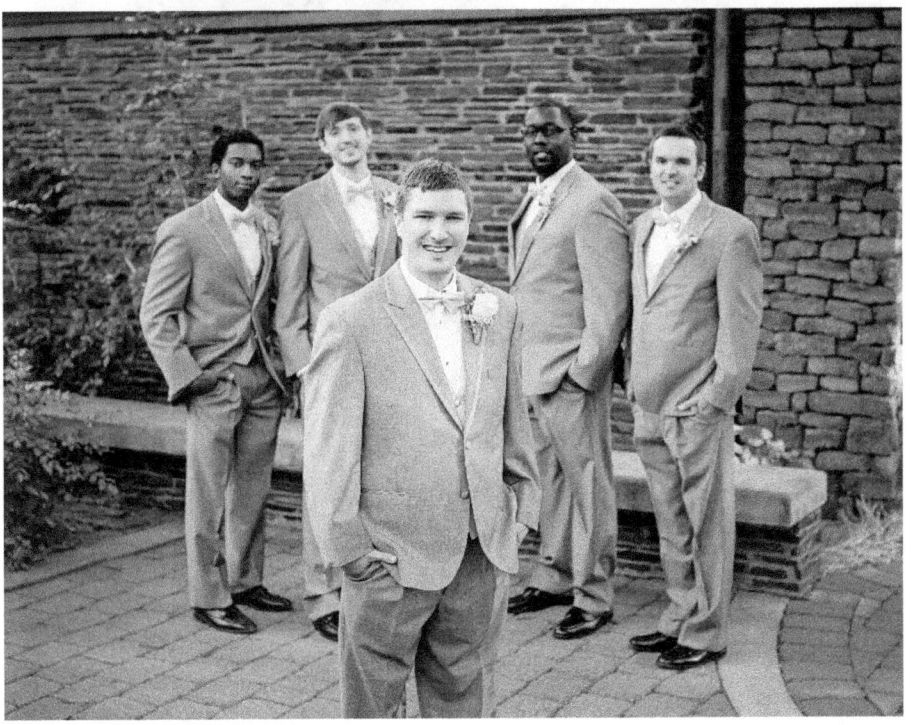

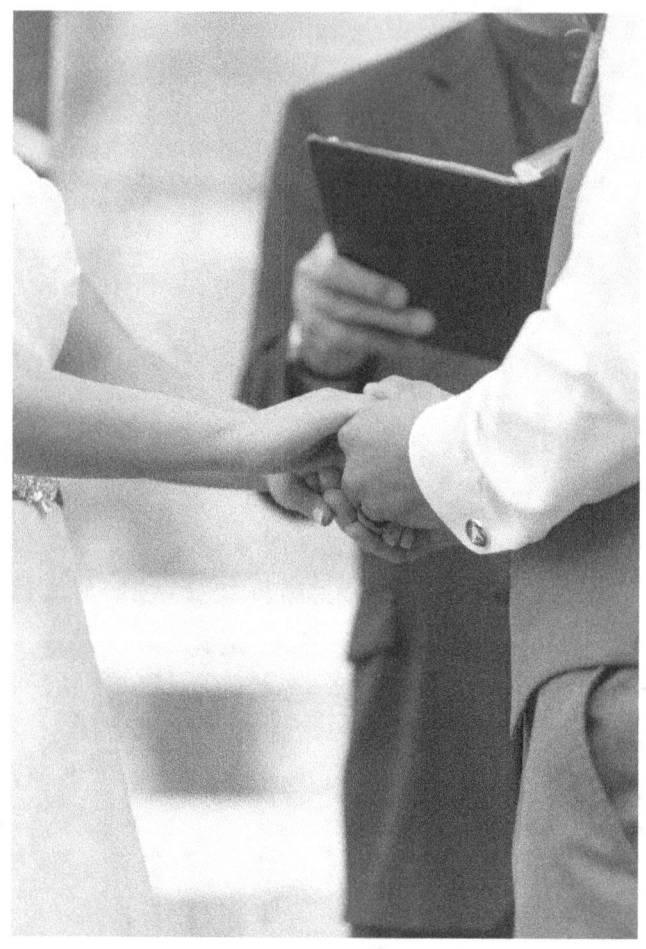

Here's an example of my perspective from kneeling up front.

Notice the Star Trek cuff link? Make sure to capture those tiny details that show the unique personalities of the couple!

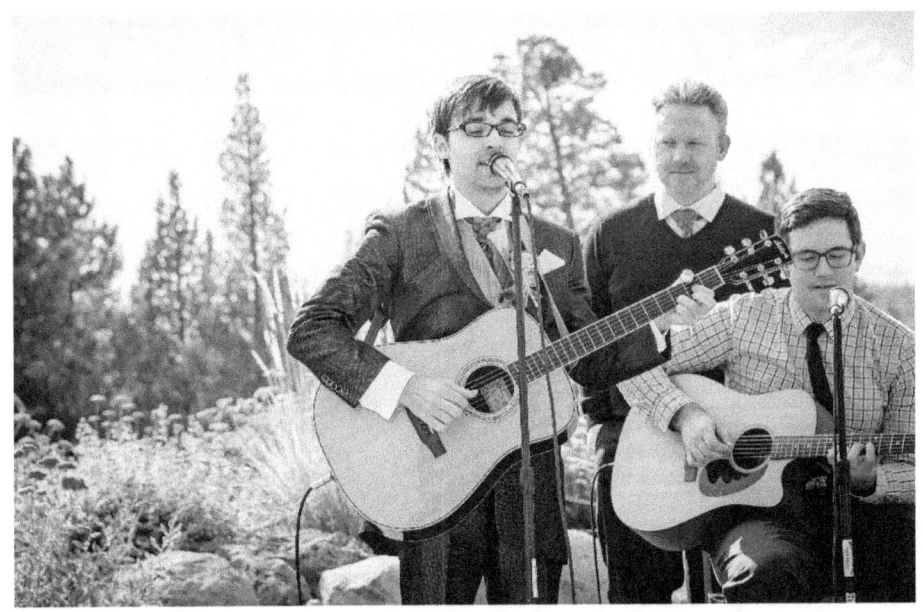

The groom at this wedding sang a song during the ceremony, that he'd written for his bride.

Sometimes there isn't room for me to be up front, so I'll shoot from farther back, (left) or as in this outdoor wedding (right) I'll circle around and shoot from other angles.

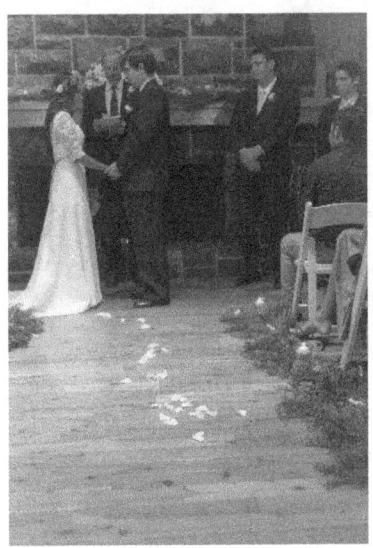

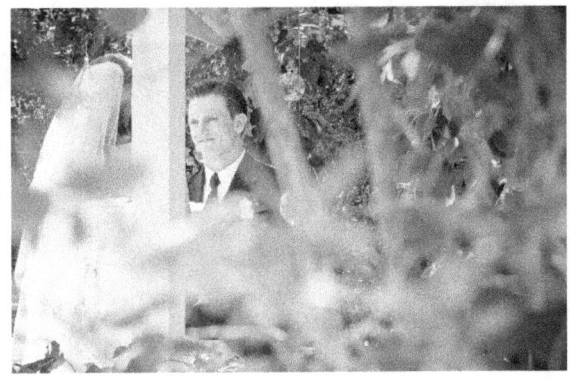

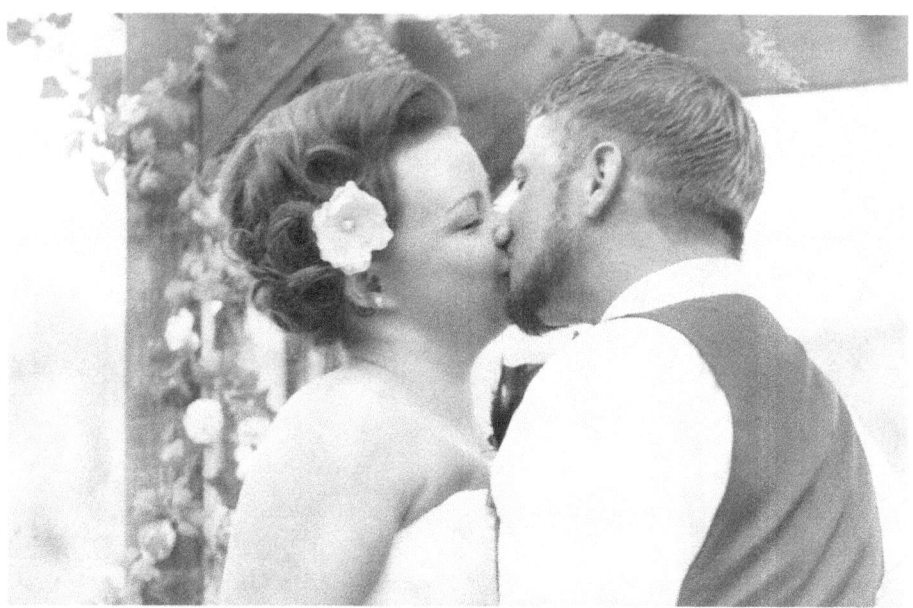

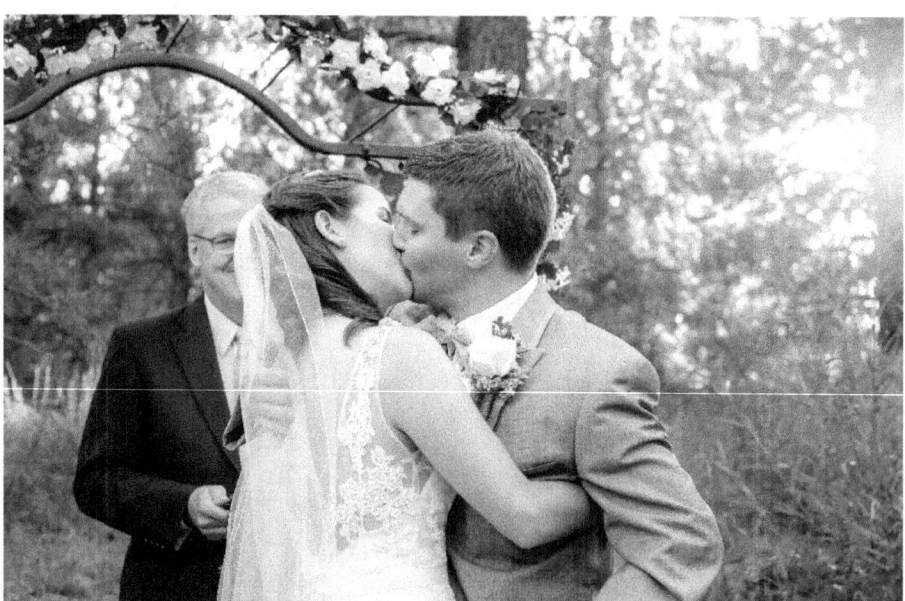

For the kiss, it's a good idea to let the couple know before the ceremony that they should make it a nice long one! That ensures that you won't miss it, and might even give you time for several shots at different focal lengths.

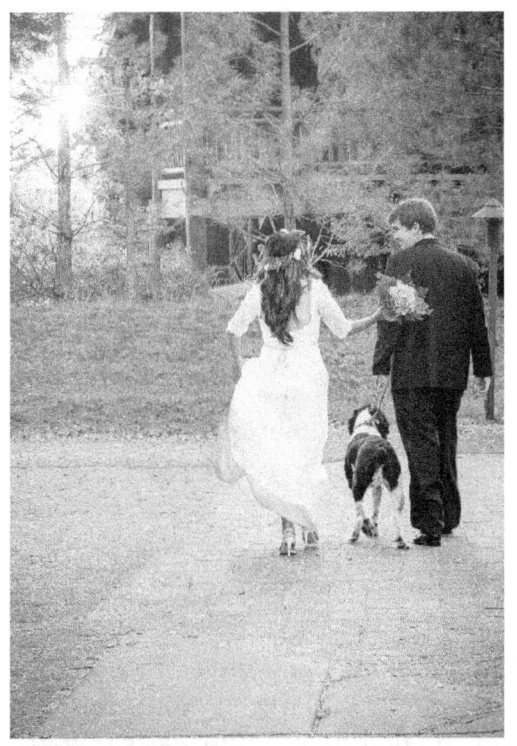

Here are a couple examples of photos that I take to show a transition in the story. It might be an image of the couple leaving the ceremony or arriving at the reception, or walking from the reception to an outdoor photo location. These images can be used in the album to show the reader that the scene is changing.

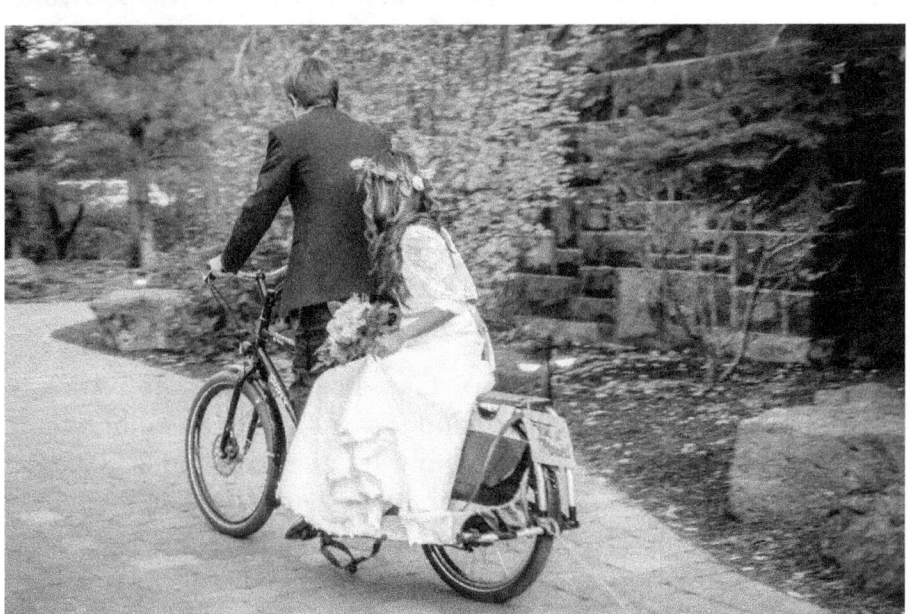

Chapter Five

Helpful Tips

--Second Looks and Panic-Busters—

    I wanted to add a little more to the subject of the First Look. Although it may fly in the face of all that's been conventional for many years, I highly recommend it!

    The beauty of a first look is that it allows us to do all the bridal party pictures with the bride and groom before the ceremony, saving so much time later when things are busier, and allowing the couple to join the reception much sooner.

    Some brides still insist on waiting until the ceremony, wanting the groom to see her for the first time as she walks toward him down the aisle. There is an expectation that the groom's face will light up with joy, and that photo of him will become a priceless treasure.

    However, the reality is that I've never once seen this happen! The groom is usually too stressed, or nervous, or even too emotional to have any look on his face other than grim determination, a blank stare, or maybe a calm smile.

    Now, I'm not saying it can't happen, but it's not as likely as the bride may hope.

    The truth is, if the first look takes place in a private setting, when they're both more relaxed and focused, then the emotion and happiness is much more likely to show in their expressions. Plus, the special moment of seeing the bride walking toward him down the aisle is not diminished if he saw her 30 minutes earlier. There is a magic to that sight that he'll never forget, even if it doesn't show on his face!

Keeping things as stress-free and moving smoothly as possible is part of our job description. The more relaxed the couple is (as much as can be possible on such a stressful day!) the more genuine the emotions will be in the photos.

A wedding is vastly different from any portfolio-building sessions you have done. Even if you're armed with all the right equipment, your assistant/second shooter, and loads of skill and confidence radiating from you at every turn, there's still that one underlying truth that haunts every moment: this can never be re-done if you mess up!

A wedding is a one-shot deal, there are no do-overs. If you miss something, it's gone in an instant.

So when we're shooting and we know that pressure is there, there can be a tendency at first to simply go blank! The mind searches frantically for the right thing to do next, and you stand there just knowing that you're forgetting something important.

Something that's really helpful for those moments of panic (especially for your first year) is a shot list.

You can keep it in your camera bag, or your pocket, and pull it out to quickly scan during a quiet moment. That way you know you won't leave out anything important, like a picture of the wedding cake before it was cut, or the bride with just her maid of honor during the bridal party shots.

There's a sample shot list at the end of the book, feel free to add to it as you like!

Once you've done enough weddings to have the list memorized, you'll find yourself referring to it less and less. You won't panic anymore, and the whole process will become more streamlined.

Also, I like to go over the list with the bride before the wedding. That way if there's anything specific that she wants to add, or something for a certain cultural or religious ceremony that isn't typical, we'll make sure to include it.

Pinterest can be helpful as well when you're starting to shoot weddings. Look for bridal portraits, detail shots, couple's poses, family groups, and anything else you might think is helpful.

You can even print out "posing cards" to have on hand, but only when you're still portfolio-building or doing sessions with friends. During an actual wedding you won't to stop and go through a stack of printed poses, or pull out your phone to go through your Pinterest boards!

I know, many photographers hate Pinterest with a passion. They can't stand it when bride says "Oh, I saw this amazing photo on Pinterest, can you do this?"

Instead of giving her a speech about my creativity (and how I want to come up with stuff that will become the newest trend on Pinterest!) I'll take the time to ask her what it is about the pictures that she specifically loves. It might be the black and white processing, the angle of the portrait, or the color scheme that drew her eye. That helps give me a feel for her style preferences in general, and I can pull in those elements instead of literally recreating a Pinterest photo.

If the bride really does want the exact photo recreated as closely as possible, I'll consider it if it's within the scope of what we're already shooting. I always get plenty of images at a wedding that showcase my unique style and creativity, so I don't mind if a bride has her heart set on one or two Pinterest copies.

You have to keep in mind that brides will most likely be spending hours and hours on Pinterest when planning their wedding, so it's not uncommon for her to become emotionally attached to a certain image that she simply *must* have!

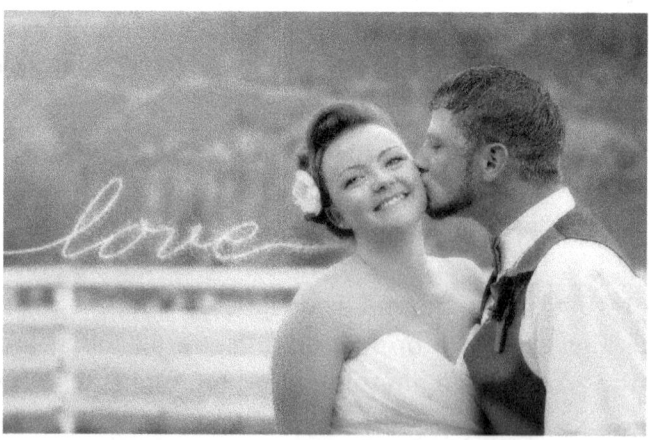

A wedding day timeline is also invaluable. This is something to go over with your bride before the big day, and make sure she has a realistic view of how much time all the pictures will take.

If they've booked you for four hours or ten hours, the timeline will obviously differ. If time is short, make sure the couple knows that they'll need to cut the cake right after dinner, and do the bouquet toss and first dance right off the bat.

Having a timeline in place for the day will help keep you from going crazy when the first dance needs to start at 8:00pm, and you're impatiently tapping your toe on the sidelines still waiting for it to start at 9:30.

Coordinate with the DJ as well, so he/she knows to keep the timeline moving briskly along.

Not many couples these days opt for an "unplugged" wedding, but it's worth suggesting. One of the main gripes on all forums for wedding photographers is the constant annoyance of 'Uncle Bob' or 'Aunt Mary', those guests that step right in front of the pro and block the all-important shot of the first kiss, or anything else!

It's understandable that the happy couple wants to have a lot of pictures, and may not mind at all that their friends and family are all snapping away on their phones from the audience or anywhere else. But at least let them know ahead of time that the pictures you take of their ceremony will look much nicer if the guests are asked to keep their devices put away until the reception.

I have a clause in my contract that states I am not responsible for missing any shots if another guest with a camera gets in the way. It does happen! If I have time, I can politely tap them on the shoulder and ask if they could move for just a moment, but there isn't always time.

When this happens, I make sure to take a picture anyway, even if all it shows is Uncle Bob's back right in front of me. That way if the bride asks why we didn't get a shot of her and her hubby kissing on the dance floor, I can show her that picture and politely point out that I did try, but this guest got right in front of me when it happened.

When I was first starting out, I had a cake cutting completely ruined when a flock of guests gathered all around me with cameras, and I found myself surrounded by constant flashes going off. The results were over exposed, grainy and very poor quality. I didn't have the time to stop everything and ask the guests to please wait so I could get the pictures that the bride and groom were paying me to get.

I also had a bride once who kept saying "the more pictures the better!" as various guests got in my way, or actually tried to take over my job! One guest in particular was...um...difficult to work with. She was a pro photographer from out of state (and should have known better) and she brought along *all* her gear.

She would move importantly around, giving directions and taking pictures (dismissing groups before I had even gotten my shots!), then herded the newlyweds off for a private session as the last light was fading.

I don't know if I've ever been more frustrated at a wedding, but since she was a friend of the family and the bride seemed to be enjoying every minute I kept my mouth shut.

I refused to be pushed aside however, (even if the officiant thought she was the 'official' photographer at first!) and I kept calm and tried my best to get the shots I needed.

Fortunately, I love a challenge! I'm one of those people who thrives on them, and will work three times harder to come up with a way to overcome.

When I was waiting for the bouquet toss, as the sun was setting and we were about to lose our outdoor light in the deep canyon setting, that lady slipped off around the other side of the building with the couple for that private session.

Fortunately, my husband was assisting me at that wedding, and he happened to see what was going on and came quickly to let me know.

I ran off in their direction with my 70-200, and finally saw them in the distance, standing against a fence with the beautiful sunset behind them.

Now, that sunset was completely unexpected! We couldn't see that side of the sky from the reception, although I had been checking off and on and it seemed as though the clouds would be too heavy for any pretty sunset pictures.

But my 'competition' had caught sight of that last moment of sunlight that burst into gorgeous reds and purples, and instead of telling me, she had taken the couple to get her own pictures.

I stayed farther back and took pictures of them at 200mm. She was standing literally right in front of them, getting more close-up shots. I knew if I could stay off to one side (just enough to keep her out of the frame) and shoot the whole scene, that it would be beautiful. I shot from low down, got that whole amazing sky into the picture, and out of the dozens that I shot I got one that was really amazing!

I had to clone the other lady's body out of part of the scene, but it was worth the effort. I ended up gifting that image as a 16x20 metallic print to the couple, and they were blown away!

After that happened, I added an exclusivity clause to my contract, stating that I will be the only professional photographing the wedding. It also showed me that the profession I had chosen was bound to be a stressful one at times!

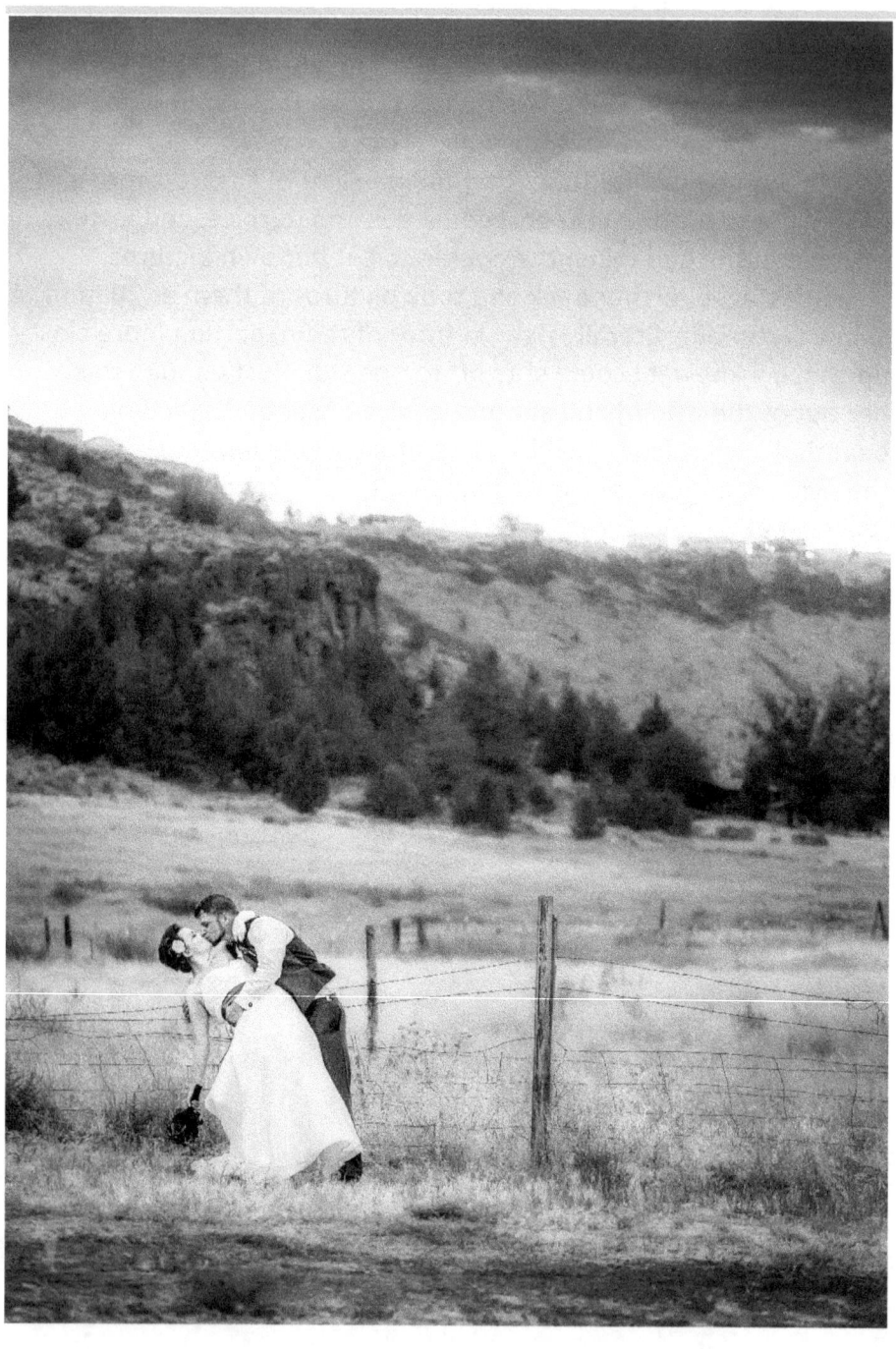

Chapter Six

Post Processing

--After the Ball—

Now let's talk about your post-processing workflow. You finish shooting a wedding and get home exhausted, put your camera bag away and fall into bed. Right?

No, I'm afraid your day isn't over yet! I never leave the wedding pictures on the memory card overnight. I'll make sure to upload them to Lightroom and put backup copies on an external hard drive.

I prefer to use a USB cable to connect my camera to the computer, rather than using a card reader. I once heard that you're less likely to have problems that way, so that's what I did and it became a habit! Whatever your method, you should have all the pictures in three places (memory cards, computer and external hard drive) before you go to bed.

Lightroom and Photoshop are both available as a set for $9.99 a month from Adobe. Using the monthly subscription method is an easy, inexpensive option that lets you get any future upgrades for free.

There are many good tutorials on Youtube and great books on the subject of photo editing, and you will develop your own unique style over time. Rather than getting into the specifics of editing styles, I want to go over my post-wedding workflow.

One of the best Lightroom workflow tutorials is demonstrated by Aaron Nace of Phlearn. If you're just getting started with Lightroom and Photoshop, most of his tutorials will be too advanced for you right now, but the video on workflow will be really helpful! He explains the most organized way to download and keep track of your photos from each session. Look for it at: **https://www.youtube.com/watch?v=dU5XweqovMQ**

Once I have all images uploaded to LR, I go through them (the next morning) and quickly give 1 star to each 'keeper'. Many find the culling process to be time consuming, and hard to get through. It can be challenging to know which pictures to keep, and which to toss.

I keep at least two almost-identical pictures of each family group shot, in case somebody had their eyes closed or wasn't smiling. That way I can do a head-swap later on.

The images I absolutely love get two stars, and I'll finish editing these first and post some as a sneak peek on Facebook and use them in the blog post.

Once I've gone through the images, only marking with a star the ones I want to keep, I filter for 'rated' images, which leaves only the pictures with at least one star. Now I can go into the Develop module and start on the first image.

(I recently learned about using Photo Mechanic to cull images, and that it's much faster. I plan to try this with my next wedding!)

The fastest way to edit in Lightroom is in batches. Make the changes you want on the first image in a set (same location, same lighting). Then highlight the other pictures in the set by holding down the shift key and clicking the last image in the row.

Then click the Sync button in the lower right corner. This brings up a dialog box with many options to check or uncheck. Those are the edits that will be copied to all the other images you selected, so if you cropped the first image and don't want the same crop applied to all of them, make sure to uncheck 'crop'.

When you're ready, click OK and watch the magic happen!

Editing in batches like this will cut your editing time drastically! I used to take every single image into Photoshop and edit them even more, making each one as perfect as I could as if it was for a magazine.

This was taking so much time, I was literally spending over 100 hours editing one wedding! My husband suggested I find a faster way to do it or outsource my editing. I always enjoyed editing and didn't want to give that up, so I came up with the method I use now.

After editing everything in Lightroom, I select 10-15 images to open in Photoshop. I know some photographers let their clients choose their favorite pictures to receive that extra editing, but I usually choose them myself and wait to let the client see them when they're all finished.

I try to post a sneak peek on Facebook the day after the wedding, or within the next two days. This should be 3-4 images with your watermark. Don't forget to tag your clients, and encourage them to tag friends and family.

At the consultation, I will typically give the bride a timeline of a week for the first sneak peeks, knowing that I'll get it done much faster. That gives me a buffer if I need it, but it also makes the bride feel like her wedding was just *so* amazing that I couldn't wait to share it!

One week after the wedding, I'll write up the blog post. This may seem very quick to some, but I try to have all the pictures finished within two weeks, four if I'm really busy. Remember, I edited those special images first, so the blog doesn't have to wait until all the pictures are done.

So now I have my edited pictures, ready to upload onto my client's gallery. How many images should you deliver to your client anyway? That number will vary widely depending on who you ask, but most photographers will end up with about 100 photos per hour of shooting. Weddings with a lot of details and many special events during the day will naturally have more.

Please, whatever you do, do not give your clients all the unedited photos on a disc. Many beginning photographers will do this "shoot and burn" method to save time and money, but it's not a viable business plan for long term.

Part of your client's motivation to hire you should be the unique artistic style of your work. Never show them unedited photos! If you decide to let them select the images that you will process with Photoshop, you should still give them all a basic edit in LR first.

Now, send an email to your happy couple to let them know that their photos are ready! Unless of course you do IPS (in person sales), in which case you'll have them come into your studio or home to go over the pictures with you.

IPS can bring in more income, if you have the room for it. It allows you to have a relaxing environment, candles, drinks, soft jazz, chocolates, and the wedding images playing as a slideshow on a big screen. The couple remembers the emotion and happiness of their wedding, and when you bring out samples that are available for them to purchase a la carte, they'll be more likely to make additional purchases.

You don't have to be pushy or put pressure on a couple during IPS. No one appreciates that, and you don't want to make them spend more than they're comfortable with. That won't get you any referrals!

If you're not doing IPS, then you just need to complete the items that your couple paid for when they booked you. It might be a pre-selected number of prints, a canvas, album, or USB with their digital files. Whatever it is, you only need to get them ordered, package them attractively and ship or deliver them to your client. And you're done!

--Album Design—

I typically use Miller Labs for my client's prints and canvases. The quality is outstanding, and I've had nothing but amazing customer service with them.

I use GraphiStudio.com for all my albums. They're handmade in Italy, and of the highest quality you can find anywhere. My smallest package includes the 8x8 boxed album with 20 pages.

I include an album with all my collections, since the purpose of my wedding photography is after all to tell a story. And what's a story without a book?

Remember how I said that I try to shoot with the album in mind? Make sure to include some 'wow' shots for impact, especially for the final image in the album. Keep the layout clean and simple, and tell the story from start to finish.

Here's how my layout for a 20-page album typically comes together:

Page 1: Bride getting hair/make up done
Page 2-3: Detail shots of the shoes, jewelry, flowers
Page 4-5: Bride getting dressed
Page 6-7: Ceremony begins, flower girl/ring bearer
Page 8-9: Bridal party enters, Bride enters
Page 10-11: The vows, exchanging rings
Page 12-13: Candle lighting, sand pouring, any meaningful element, first kiss
Page 14-15: Bridal party pictures
Page 16-17: Family photos
Page 18-19: First dance, cake cutting
Page 20: a WOW image of bride and groom

Of course, I prefer to have more pages to work with, as I can fit in so many more elements of their unique story. Since I don't want pages that are cluttered with lots of little pictures, having 20 pages means I only get to use 30 or so images.

When designing the album, I've found that my clients usually want me to put it together myself, rather than having to choose all the pictures on their own.

I'll put together a first draft, and send the bride an email with thumbnail images of the layout. Once she looks at it, she'll get back to me with any changes she wants and I'll send her the final draft when it's ready.

It's usually easier this way, and less stress for the brides who may not know which pictures will look best in the album. They still get to make sure their favorite images are included, and give approval for the final layout before I send it to the printer.

You will probably want to add in a surprise gift for the couple; something they weren't expecting that will make them want to sing your praises! I select one of the nicest images, and make it into a printed canvas or a stunning metallic 16x20 print.

When I was first starting out, I opted for less expensive options like a small set of thank you cards or an 8x10 print mounted on styrene with a pearl finish.

Another way to give your client an unexpected gift is to add on extra album spreads. If you sell extra pages as an add-on or a la carte option at a high price, then they will appreciate the value of getting those pages for free. This will have very little added cost for you, with a high perceived value to your clients!

One way to do this is to say "You had so many amazing images from your wedding, I just had to add on five extra spreads to your album. I'd love to give you those extra pages as my gift to you." And make sure to include them with the other pages for her approval before printing.

When the photos are all ready, and you give your clients the first draft album pages, you could also give them a coupon for 50% off prints. They can use this to order as many prints as they like, but it must be used before the album is submitted for printing.

This adds some incentive to order prints right away!

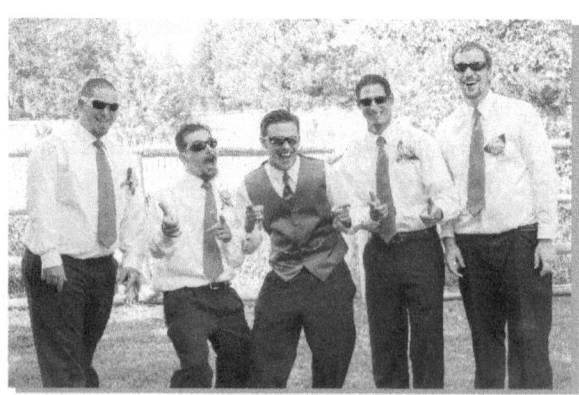

Chapter Seven

Branding, Marketing and Pricing

--Defining Brand—

First of all, "branding" is not the same as "marketing". It's not about passing out cards, writing an info packet, producing a studio magazine, mailing sales flyers or getting a really great profile photo or yourself. Branding is more of an 'image', the feeling that your business projects. When you think of certain well-known brands, you have distinct impressions of what their brand 'means' to you.

Your brand is all the elements of your business working together to project the right image to your clients.

This branding process can take time, as you grow your business and figure out exactly what you want your brand to portray. To get started, sit down right now and write down three words that you feel best describe your style.

Some options are: natural, soft, warm, fun, creative, passionate, modern, bright, colorful, vintage, relaxed, artistic, classic, intimate, carefree, lavish.

When you have chosen the three that best describe your style, then put those words on the wall above your desk. Make sure all the elements of your business reflect those words. The images in your portfolio, your cards, your business colors, even the style of wording on your website should fit these defining words.

Keep your three words in mind when you shoot! When doing an engagement session for example, make sure your focus is on capturing images that are "warm, intimate and artistic" (those are my words, use your own!)

Having this focus will help you establish your own unique brand. If you're not sure what image you're currently projecting, ask your friends and family to go to your website and choose three words from that list that they think bests describes your brand. It can be very helpful to get outside opinions!

Marketing, on the other hand, is something that most photographers always want to do more! The philosophy is: the more marketing I do, the more business I'll get. This includes constant sales promotion, discounts, gift certificates, contests, two-for-one, free prints with purchase, mini sessions, etc...

I want to make it clear that the most important thing for you to do, if you want to grow your business and bring in clients, is NOT more marketing! You should be posting photos on your Facebook business page, and write a blog post at least twice a week. Your clients should see that you're actively and constantly working, shooting and thriving.

Your blog posts don't have to all be new client sessions either. They could be personal projects, informative 'how-to' pieces, behind the scenes, before-and-after examples, stylized shoots and so on.

This doesn't mean that promoting your business is wrong. Just don't put all your focus on enticing clients with sales and special offers. Make sure there is plenty of content for them to see when they look at your blog or FB page! Sell yourself as a photographer, and prove that you have the skills to bring in clients.

I do want to talk about some elements of marketing and promotion that I use. I have three magazines that I made, both in print and online. One is my wedding magazine, and it covers my pricing, some basic Q&A, info about myself and my business, as well as what clients should expect if they decide to hire me. I send this out to brides who may be interested in my services but want more information, and I also include it in my welcome packet.

You can take a look at:

http://www.magcloud.com/browse/issue/988222?__r=573906

Having a magazine with your own photos and lots of helpful information is a great way to keep yourself at the top of a bride's list of prospects. A magazine has perceived value, so she's more likely to keep it than a single-page flyer or an email. Plus, it's full of lovely photos that you took, allowing her to mentally compare you to the work she's seen from other photographers.

The second magazine is a guide on 'what to wear' for family portraits. I send the link to the digital copy of this one to clients who book me for family sessions. This is always appreciated, and helps them to feel confident in my knowledge and skill to make them look their best.

The third magazine is a product catalog. This is great for sending to clients who've done any kind of session with you. It can show them how amazing their photos would look as a large wall print, or in a fun collage, and can bring in more orders.

It's even better if you do IPS, and they can flip through it while you provide actual samples of the products for them to see as well. If you don't show it, you can't sell it!

This is why sample products are so important. You should have at least one sample album when you start out, adding on various styles as you build your portfolio.

Anything you offer in a wedding collection or a la carte on your price list should be represented by an actual sample to show clients. This includes canvas prints, metal or acrylic prints, mini accordion albums, anything!

If you want to make your own magazines, you can start off with some great templates that make it really simple. I used some from Squijoo.com (you can sign up for $5 a month) and customized them in Photoshop.

I bought the template for my Glamour magazine (still a work in progress!) From BP4U. (**http://bp4uphotographerresources.com**) They're another fun resource for templates, actions and overlays.

If you're needing some inexpensive business cards to get you started, Vistaprint.com is a great place. If you want something that will really stand out, consider MillersLab.com and spend a bit more on an ornate style card. (Called the Business Luxe Card.) These have beautifully shaped edges, and will come across as more luxurious and special.

Millers is also I lab I use for prints. They provide free next-day shipping on most orders!

Any client who's interested in hiring you should be given an info packet or marketing portfolio. This should contain a business card, your pricing info, mini photo book with a selection of your best images, information about your style of shooting, and any press or awards you've won. This can all fit into a simple folder with inside pockets.

I mentioned my Welcome Packet earlier also, so let's talk about that too. When a client decides to hire me, and they sign the contract and pay the retainer fee, I send them a welcome packet.

This should contain a few basic things: a welcome letter, info on their engagement session and how to prepare for that, a tri-fold studio brochure, pricing guide, business card magnet, and maybe a hair/make up guide or wedding planner, and a wedding magazine. Then you can select a few items to add to this that reflect your brand. Some options are: scented soap, his and hers mugs (his and hers anything!) a tote bag with your studio logo, chocolates, etc...

Your new clients should be blown away, and glad that they hired someone as thoughtful as you!

Follow this up with an email containing the engagement session reminder, and tell them you can't wait to meet with them again and get some amazing engagement pictures!

After the engagement session, here's what happens next: they get an email with a link to their pictures on the website. I also create a Facebook timeline photo for them to use, which can be a great way for all their friends to see your work!

I recently found out about a company called Chasing Lockets (chasinglockets.com) that makes custom lockets for brides using an engagement picture. Sending one of those, along with a small accordion album of their best engagement images will go a long way toward making your clients feel pampered!

Two weeks before the wedding, consider sending a Starbucks gift card, with a note telling the bride and groom to take a moment and relax from all the wedding planning, and to enjoy some time together before the big day.

As far as marketing after the wedding, I produce a slide show with Animoto.com. This usually has 50 images set to a song that I feel fits the theme of the wedding. Without fail, this brings the bride to tears! They love sharing this with their friends and family, and the special memories that it brings. Of course, include your logo and website at the end of the slideshow.

--The Price is Right—

Pricing is an area that strikes fear into many hearts, and most photographers are afraid of setting their prices too high. After all, won't the cheaper photographer get the most clients?

You know you don't always buy the cheapest item on the shelf. You buy the brand that you trust, and the best quality for your money. You don't expect high quality to have the lowest price. In fact, you probably wouldn't believe it was a high quality item if it was the cheapest option!

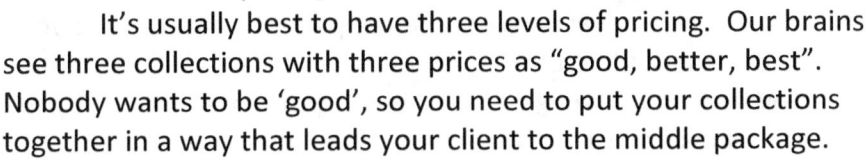

There is a perceived value with a higher price tag that can work in your favor if your prices are a little higher than the local average. However, this level of pricing must come with great quality and attention to your clients' needs. Once you feel your business has reached this level, don't be afraid to price your services accordingly.

It's usually best to have three levels of pricing. Our brains see three collections with three prices as "good, better, best". Nobody wants to be 'good', so you need to put your collections together in a way that leads your client to the middle package.

Always present your collections in descending order, with the most expensive one first. There is some psychology involved in this arrangement, since the mind sees the first price and sets a mental note of that price as the baseline or standard. Any lower priced collections that follow will be perceived as cheaper, since they're lower than the first price.

Here's an example: you walk into a camera store and see a display of prime lenses. You know you want a good quality 50mm, but you don't want to spend too much.

If the salesperson shows you the cheapest one first, your brain will latch onto that price and compare all the others to it.

"This one is $350." They tell you. It's not as nice as you wanted, but it would probably work.

Then they bring out another lens, this one is a mid-range at $500. That's a lot of money. That first one was almost as good, and lots cheaper!

The last one is the top-of-the-line lens, and you nearly fall over at the price tag that's over $1,000! You quickly decide on the cheapest lens, and congratulate yourself on saving so much money.

But what if the salesperson showed you the best lens first? They would point out all the options it had: the extra sharp focusing abilities, the beautiful bokeh, gorgeous colors and ease of use. You'd fall in love, and wish you could afford it.

The second one then would be brought out, and you'd realize it was much closer to your price range. It's not as nice as the first one, which you still love, but you know this one has the quality you need and you'd be satisfied with it in the long run.

The last lens is brought out, at the cheapest price point yet. It seems almost laughable when compared to the other two. You don't want to waste good money on something as important as a new lens, and you know you won't be happy with that one. So you decide to buy the middle one.

You end up feeling good about your purchase, knowing you chose good quality with a good price.

You can see that there's nothing sneaky or dishonest about this, we're not trying to swindle our clients! It's just a way to help them choose the best collection for their needs and make sure they know they got a good value for the price.

So you have three collections, but what do you put in them? There's quite a range of opinion, and just about every photographer will have something slightly different. As an example, here's what I offer in mine:

The Marilyn Collection - $5,299
- Up to 10 hours of wedding day coverage
- 2 Photographers
- USB drive with all wedding images
- Online gallery to view and order prints
- Engagement session and Bridal session
- Engagement guest book
- 16x12 40-page art book, crystal or leather cover
- Slideshow and custom iPhone album
- 100 thank-you cards

The Audrey Collection - $4,299
- Up to 8 hours of wedding day coverage
- 2 Photographers
- Photo CD with all wedding photos
- Online gallery to view and order prints
- Engagement session
- 10x10 30-page art book with hard cover
- Slideshow and custom iPhone album
- 100 thank-you cards

The Katherine Collection - $3,299
- Up to 6 hours of wedding day coverage
- 2 Photographers
- Online gallery to view and order prints
- Engagement session
- 8x8 20-page art book

Some photographers simply call their collections one, two and three, or silver, gold and platinum, or something simple. I chose to use names from famous actresses, since my brand is about glamour and making my brides feel like movie stars! You can come up with something that fits your brand if you choose.

You can see that the cheapest collection (and by the way, refer to them as collections and not packages.) does not include the disc or USB of their images. Most brides want the digital images, so if they wish to add that on as an a la carte option it's $750. This brings the price up to $4,049, which is almost the same as the middle collection. For only $250 more, they would get another 2 hours of coverage, a larger album and 100 cards! This is clearly a better deal.

You can see how I'm trying to steer my clients toward the middle collection. The higher priced package is there to show them how much more they could be spending! Of course, some clients might want to pay an extra thousand dollars to have the largest collection, and I hope they do! The engagement guest book is only offered with that one, and it's a great item. What couple wouldn't want a guest book that's full of their own engagement photos?

That larger collection also includes the biggest album, with the most luxurious cover options. Your sample items should include your higher-end products, which of course you show to your clients first!

As you talk through your collections, the albums get smaller, the add-ons get taken away, and they'll be more likely to want to keep the nicer options.

When starting out, your prices won't be the same as mine. I can't tell you what prices to use, but here's a good formula to start out with: figure out your cost of goods, like I did in the beginning. Add 30% to that, and there's your base price. Increase that by 10% each year.

Another rule of thumb is that you once you sell three of your most expensive collections you should raise your prices by 10%.

Something else to keep in mind is brain vs. emotion. When your clients are looking at your price list, trying to decide if they want to hire you, you want them to be in an emotional frame of mind. If their logical brain is presented with a straightforward list or spreadsheet of numbers, they'll make the logical and rational choice and select the lowest priced collection.

If that same price list is presented as an upscale menu, with a leather cover and high quality paper, and there are beautiful photos on the side of the page that they can connect with emotionally, then they're much more likely to choose a higher priced option.

Of course, there are items available a la carte, as well as in the collections. Anything that you sell should be available as a sample that your clients can see and hold.

Some ideas for additional items you can sell are: metal prints, acrylic prints, triptych canvases, parent albums (smaller sizes offered as add-ons), various sizes of prints, collage prints, accordion albums, and customized thank you cards. Make samples of all that you plan to offer (using photos that you have taken) and have them on hand to show clients, instead of simply showing them samples from the printer's website.

Remember that familiar saying: If you don't show it, you can't sell it! Here is a 100-page Primo Album from GraphiStudio.

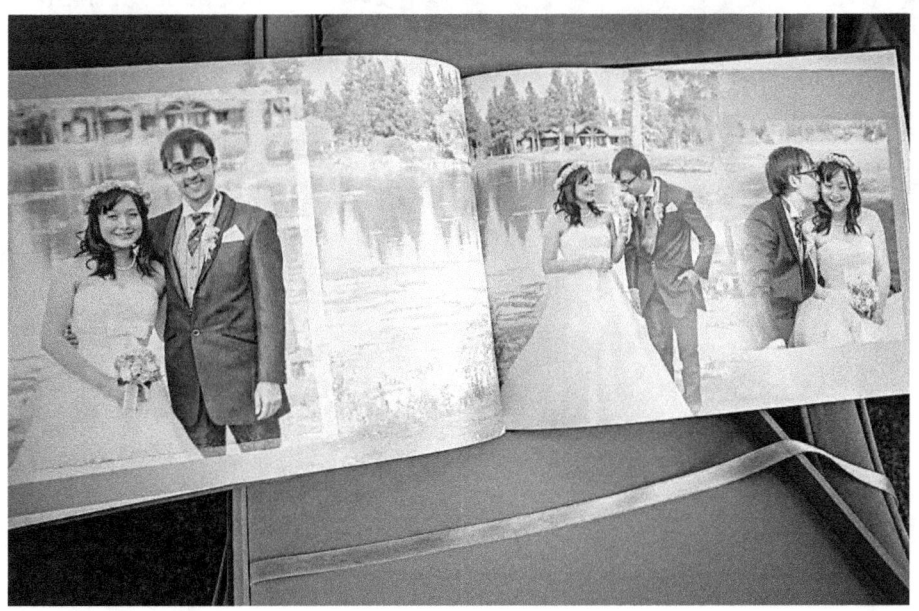

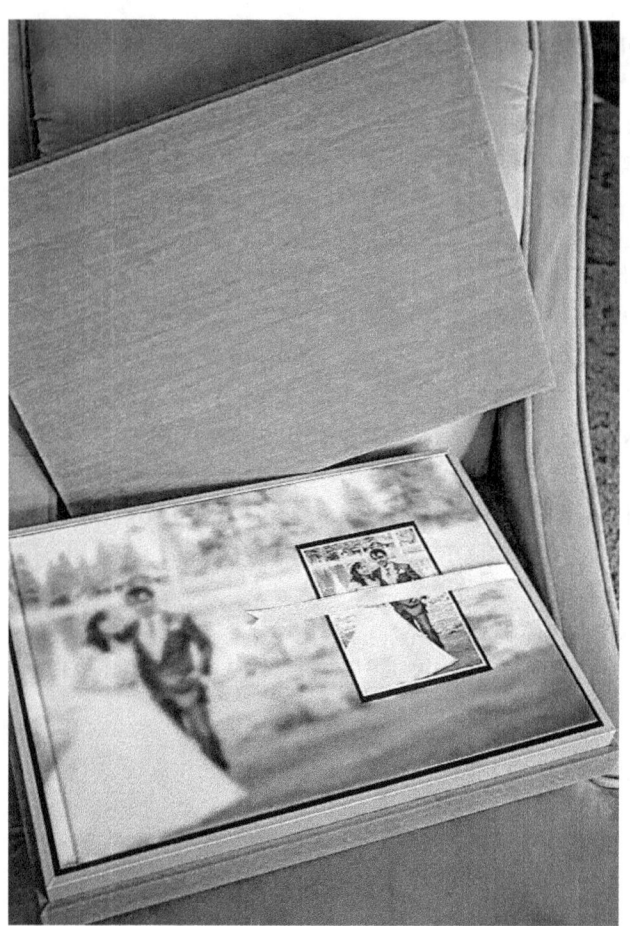

This picture shows the same 12 x 16 100-page album in its custom box. The boxes are a great way to incorporate the couple's wedding colors as well as protect the album.

Keep in mind that albums should be sold to your clients at cost x 3. So an album that costs you $150 to order should be sold to your clients at $450 to cover all your costs and leave you with a profit after taxes!

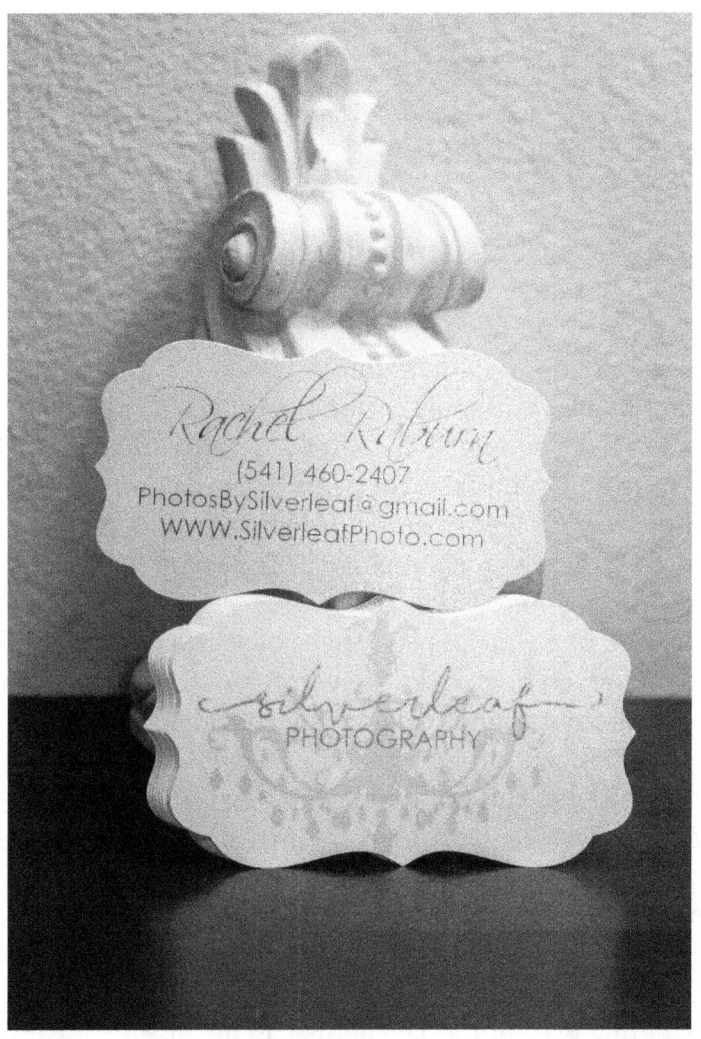

I took this shot as I was writing this book, just to show you what my business cards look like. This special edge is available from Millers lab. I have my logo on one side and my contact info on the other, and the cardstock has a pearl finish.

Chapter Eight

Client Interaction

--Booking the Wedding--

The first time you hear from a prospective client will most likely be an email, or maybe a phone call. The first question they'll probably ask will be "what are your prices?"

First of all, you should include your 'starting price' on your website. That lets people know what your base price is, so they won't have to call to find out they can't afford you. Having this information on your website (and not your complete price list) is a good way to 'pre-qualify' your clients. They won't contact you if they can't afford your base price.

Instead of giving all your prices over the phone, suggest that you meet in person to go over the whole range of options that you have to offer. Say something like: "My collections start at a similar price to other local photographers, but we have a unique style and philosophy that you can't find anywhere else. Our goal is to create a story about your wedding day, and provide you with works of art instead of just taking pictures. It's more about the experience and capturing the emotion and story of your day. I'd love to meet with you and show you what I'm talking about, and we can go over a list of prices."

Meeting with potential clients can be challenging if you don't have a studio. If you don't have a nice room in your house to use, then meeting in a coffee shop or renting a conference room are other options. The atmosphere should be professional, you should have samples to show, and be ready to listen to their plans for the wedding and what they're looking for in a photographer.

You will go over your prices and sample products (if you're meeting in a coffee shop, you don't have to bring all your samples, just some of your best albums), talk about their options and give them time to read everything.

Once you're clear what their needs are, then if necessary you can offer to create a custom collection for them. This may offer more time, or an additional album, or whatever they require. Offering to add an extra hour of coverage on the wedding day for free can be helpful for clients that are on the fence.

Remember that your time is money, so don't give away too much of it! Gifts like extra prints, additional album spreads, and other small products will have a minimal out-of-pocket cost for you, but can be wonderful incentives for your clients.

I'm not suggesting that you keep offering more and more freebies until they agree to book you! But if they need seven hours and the collection they can afford only comes with six, consider offering that hour. Or if they have their hearts set on a set of parent albums but can't afford the higher priced collection that they come with, offer to add them a la carte at a discount.

If they're hesitating, or saying that they need to talk to another family member before they book you, here's a great piece of advice: eliminate the pressure of choosing. If they're claiming to be interested in your skills as a photographer but are hesitant to commit to a collection, try this approach. Say "Once you decide that you'd like to work with us, you can pay the retainer to book your date, then decide which collection you want later on."

This can help your client feel less pressure to choose, and simply book you to secure the date. Once they hire you, go over the contract with them and have them initial and sign where needed.

When they sign, they must pay the retainer fee. Make sure to call it a retainer and not a deposit. Technically a deposit is something that can be refunded, but a retainer cannot.

The retainer is a guarantee that you will be available for them on that date, and will turn down any other requests for work on that date.

If they end up calling off the wedding, the retainer is non-refundable. If you had to turn away other jobs on that date, you lost a substantial amount of income. Some photographers offer to refund the retainer if there's enough time before the wedding for them to book another client. Once the new client is booked, the retainer from the first wedding would be refunded.

The usual amount for a retainer is 50%, but you can alter this to fit your clients' needs. For higher priced collections, I allow clients to pay less than 50% to reserve the date. I recommend not going below $500 or 50% (whichever is lower), since I've found if I let clients pay much less (like $250 on a $2,000+ collection), they end up expecting me to give them breaks later on. Those clients can be the hardest ones to please!

Your contract should state that the full balance is due no later than two weeks before the wedding. You can also offer monthly payment plans, for clients who would like to spread smaller payments over a year or more.

I have occasionally agreed to collect the final payment from a client at the wedding, but I really don't like doing this. It just feels awkward to approach a newlywed couple and ask them for a check during the reception! Plus, there's always the risk that they will have "left their checkbook at home".

Sometimes a client is anxious about getting their balance paid off in time, and they're afraid I won't come if they still owe me money. I tell them that if they're still not completely paid up by the wedding day, I will still show up and photograph the wedding. They just won't see any of their pictures until I am paid in full! (I've never had this actually happen, thankfully.) This only applies if I trust the couple, and the balance is very small.

--Engagement Session—
You've now survived your first client meeting, and hopefully booked a wedding! The next time you meet with your couple will be at the engagement session.

I require my wedding clients to have an engagement session with me, even if they've already had one done by someone else. It's included in all three of my collections, and I *strongly* urge them to take advantage of it!

This session is a great opportunity for them to become comfortable working with me, and to get familiar with some basic poses that we'll use again on the wedding day.

It also helps me to get a sense of their preferences and personalities. This knowledge helps me out a lot on the wedding day!

If a couple wants to save money, and asks me at the time of booking if they can get a collection cheaper without the engagement session, my answer is "No, the session is complimentary and not included in the price of the collection."

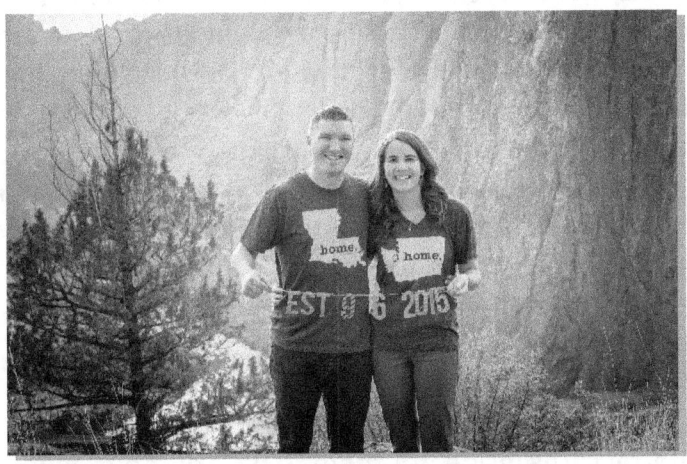

Once the session is done, you probably won't see them again until the wedding day. Keeping in touch with the gifts I mentioned earlier will be a great tool in maintaining a positive relationship.

If you choose to utilize IPS (in person sales) then you'll meet with them at least once after the wedding. Again, if you do this, have plenty of samples made of all the products that you offer.

When your clients arrive, you should have soft music playing, a scented candle burning, and champagne or other beverage available. Give them time to watch a slideshow on a big screen of all the wedding pictures.

Then give them the a la carte price list, and let them look at your sample products. You do not need to go over the prices with them, just let them look at the list.

Give them the 50% off prints coupon, and an order form for prints (if they're going to order prints from you directly and not from your website), otherwise give them a coupon with a code for 50% off prints from the website.

Remember the coupon is only valid until the album has been ordered, which is usually two weeks for me.

If they chose to order extra products, write down the order and collect payment. Listening to what they really like when going over your products can also give you a great idea for their gift!

The last time I see a client is when I deliver their album and other products they ordered. Of course I also give them their surprise gift! Any prints they ordered will be presented in an image box. You can order these from ArtsyCouture or Millers Lab. If they ordered a USB or CD, these will be packaged attractively as well.

If delivering digital images, be sure to include a print release. I made a tri-fold release form that can fit inside a CD case or accompany a USB case.

When I put together the box of items to deliver (or ship) to the client, I always include a hand-written thank you note. I tuck several referral cards inside, for them to pass out to friends.

--Other Info--

Another topic that comes up among photographers is what to wear to client meetings. At our first meeting, I try to wear something similar to what I'd wear while shooting their wedding. That way they can easily picture me in that role!

For meetings as well as at weddings I always stick with simple, professional wardrobe staples: black slacks and a black and white silk blouse, or a sleeveless black and white dress with a black cardigan. Flat black shoes, simple hair style, nothing that seems over-the-top or distracting in any way.

It's best to avoid wearing white while shooting a wedding (or attending one, for that matter!). Bright colors that draw attention to yourself aren't a good idea either.

Honestly, finding really comfortable flat shoes that won't hurt your feet after standing in them all day is one of the most important details in a wedding photographer's wardrobe!

In preparation for your first meeting with a client, it doesn't hurt to go online and find some lists that your client may very well bring with her. There are so many wedding-related websites out there, full of articles like "25 Questions to Ask Your Wedding Photographer".

You should be prepared and come up with answers to those potential questions ahead of time. You don't want to sit there blinking when the bride starts firing off questions!

Some of the most common questions I've heard are: How long have you been in business? What is your style? What kind of camera do you use? Do you have a back-up photographer in case you get sick? Do you bring studio lights? How many pictures do you take/How many pictures will I get? How many weddings have you done?

Let's talk about some of those. It's a very good idea to have another wedding photographer in your area that you can coordinate with. Someone with a shooting style similar to your own, who can step in for you in case of an emergency.

In my years of business, I've never had to miss a wedding, but it helps brides feel better to know I have a backup plan.

The question of lighting comes up from time to time. I do not bring studio lights to set up for portraits at weddings, and I inform the brides that I will use off-camera flash as needed but I get 90% of the images I take with natural light.

The question about the number of images that I take and/or deliver is a very common one. I explain to clients that I average 100 images per hour, but I do not have a minimum number that I guarantee. They will not receive every image that I take, but I assure them that I only cull out "duplicates, images that are blurry or poorly focused, or group shots where someone blinked or made a weird face."

They want to be certain that they aren't missing out on any important pictures, and that explanation usually helps to reassure them.

I do not give or sell the unprocessed RAW files at any time or for any reason. Most brides wouldn't have the software or the knowledge to process them anyway, but that's not the only reason. Remember I said earlier that your clients should want to hire you based on your unique artistic skill and vision? Your images will have their own 'look' that sets your work apart from other photographers. Giving out the RAW files is like a chef giving out the ingredients to a meal instead of preparing it. It won't be the same!

This covers most of what you'll need to know for client interaction. I hope you feel more confident now, and able to help your business grow into a huge success!

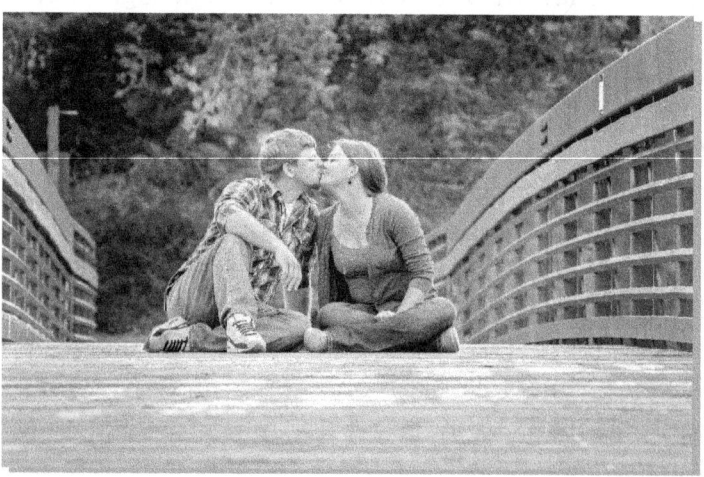

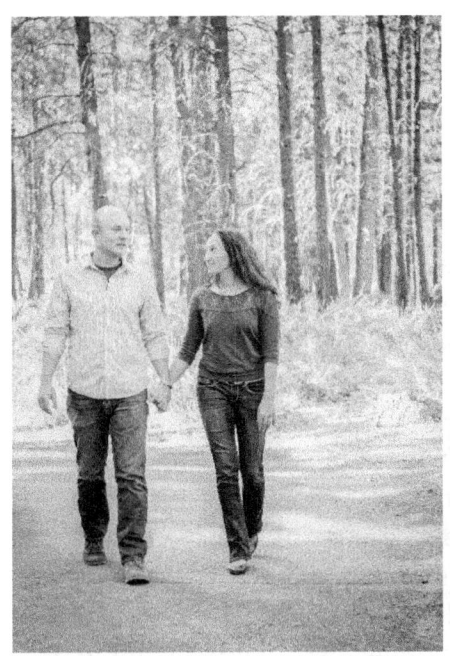
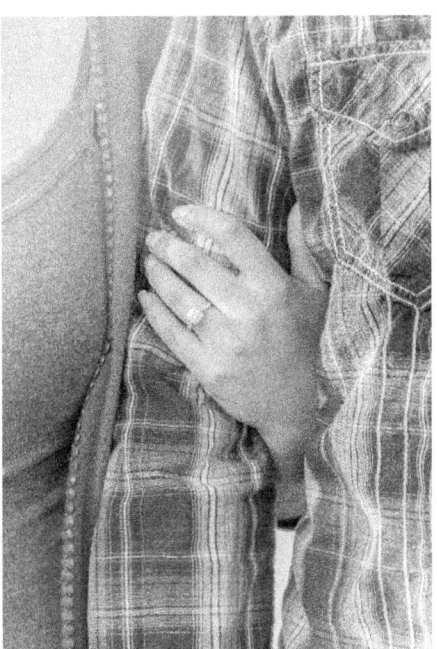
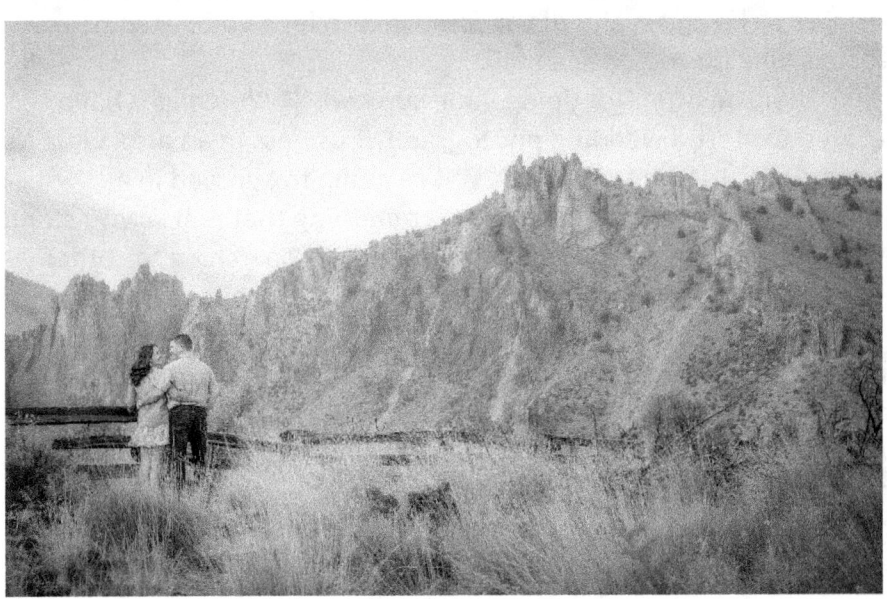

Chapter 9

You Can't Fail

If you follow all the steps we've gone over so far, you will have started a wonderful and successful photography business! I wanted to start this chapter by reminding you of my inspiration from the beginning of the book: You can't fail if you keep trying!

As long as you keep going, and keep taking pictures and posting on your blog, and never quitting, then you simply cannot fail. I'm not guaranteeing a get-rich-quick business plan, or telling you that you'll always have scores of clients flooding your inbox. I'm saying that as long as you persevere and don't throw in the towel, you'll continue to grow and succeed.

30% of new businesses fail in the first two years, and 50% have closed their doors at the end of five years. I don't want your business to be a casualty of that statistic, so let's go over some reasons why businesses can fail.

Reason one: Not doing your homework. You might have decided to start a wedding photography business in an area with 73 others doing the same thing. If you're going to succeed in a saturated market, you need to find something that makes you stand out from the crowd. Spend some time online searching for other photographers in your area, and look at their websites.

I'm not saying you should copy the ideas of the ones who charge the most and hope it works for you too! But get a feel for their styles and what they offer in their packages, then come up with an angle of your own that you can advertise on your website that will set you apart.

Please, don't pretend to be a bride and write to your competition to get all their price lists! Just browse their websites and see if there's a 'hole' that you can fill.

Sometimes your unique style will be what draws a bride's attention. I know another wedding photographer with a very unique business name that has gotten clients just because they were intrigued by the name alone!

Look for a niche that you can fill, by appealing to a narrow segment of the population, and capitalize on that.

Reason two: Not having a business plan. You can't just wake up in the morning and say to yourself "hey, I think I'm going to start a business today!"

I'm sure you realize that a lot of planning and calculating must be done first, to make sure you're ready for all that goes along with starting a business.

You should figure out all the starting expenses, how much time you'll be spending away from your family, any taxes that may apply to you, and what your goals are.

You should have a plan for where you want your business to be in one year, five years, and ten years. Have a view of the big picture, and a plan in place to make it happen.

Reason three: Too much debt. If you have to take out a loan to start your business, (which I would *strongly* advise against) you will put yourself in a risky position from square one. Without enough business coming in to cover your expenses, you'll end up spiraling downward very quickly. If things don't work out, or you decide this isn't the business for you, you could be stuck with a lot of debt and no income to repay it.

This kind of business can be started with very basic equipment, and then upgraded as you go. I'd very strongly urge you to use this method and pay as you go, instead of taking out a loan to get started. It's just not worth the extra stress.

Reason four: Ignoring your website and social media. So much about your business depends on what your clients can see about you online, it's perilous to think you can ignore it and still keep growing.

Keeping up with your blog, and posting regularly on your Facebook page are vitally important! Set an alarm on your phone to remind you when it's time to blog, Instagram, and post to your business FB page, until it becomes a habit.

Reason five: Failing to keep up with the times. Twenty years ago, what worked for a photography business will not be what works today. Your clients' needs and desires will change based on current fashion and trends. If there's a hot new trend that you avoid because you want your business to stay unchanged, you could lose a lot of business.

I'd suggest joining some Facebook groups that discuss wedding photography, join a local business association, stay active in your community and the local wedding market in general.

Taking classes online is a great way to stay up-to-date. CreativeLive.com is a fantastic resource, in fact I'd say it's far superior to any other site that I've found that offers continuing education for photographers.

There are general knowledge classes that teach the basics of using your camera, post processing, shooting engagement sessions, posing, lighting, even step-by-step classes that go through shooting an entire (real) wedding beginning to end.

For amazing classes on wedding photography specifically, look for classes taught by Susan Stripling and Jasmine Star.

I'd also recommend keeping up with some fun personal projects alongside your business work. Especially when things are slow, it's good to have something to do to keep your skills sharp.

There are many lists you can find online of 30-day challenges or something similar. Or come up with your own project.

Some projects I've done include: macro photography, looking for textures all around the house to use as overlays, composite images, different lighting effects, landscapes, creating double exposures in Photoshop, shooting panoramas and stitching the many images together in Photoshop, still life photography, and anything else that will improve or increase my skills.

Build up a good library of photography books, and keep one by your bed or in your bag when you travel.

I know that I can't possibly cover every aspect of this business in one short book, but my goal here has been to give a clear picture of the many aspects you'll need to consider.

I hope that you feel encouraged at this point, and energized to get started with your business! If you've been inspired and are able to create a successful business, I'd love to hear about it!

The community of wedding photographers are mostly very helpful and encouraging, and we want to help each other to grow. Instead of seeing each other as 'competition', we know that each of our businesses is unique and will appeal to different clients.

I sincerely want you to succeed and love what you do! So let's all work together to build each other up, and offer support and advice wherever we can!

Here's to many years of telling stories that will live forever...

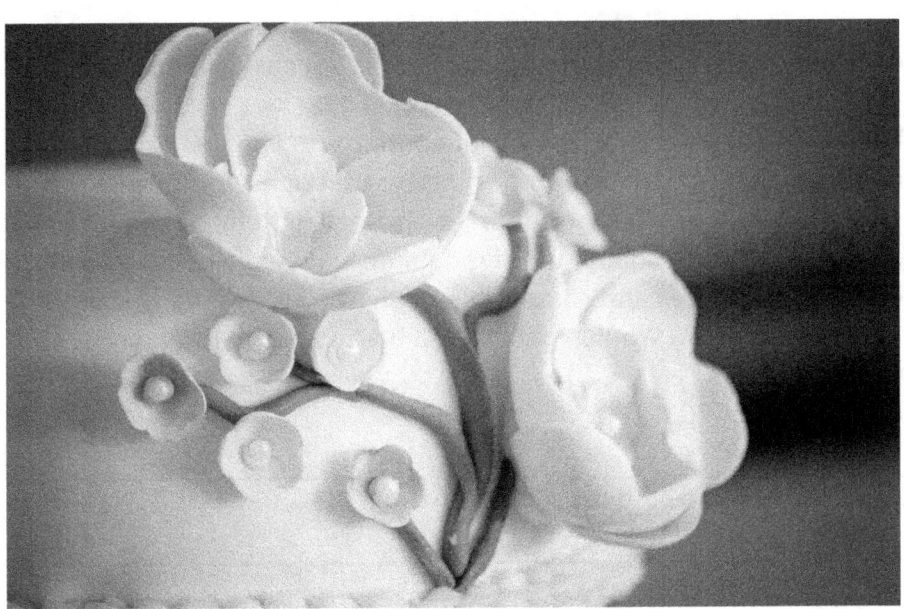

Chapter Ten

Resources

Second Shooter Sample Contract

Silverleaf Photography Agent
Silverleaf Photography, an Oregon business, hereby hires the undersigned photographer (hereinafter known as "Agent") to photograph material for Silverleaf on the following terms and conditions: Silverleaf will have full ownership of the resulting photographs including all rights to copyright in the same with no restrictions on its use except as may be set forth in the space below.

Silverleaf Photography grants the agent a license to include the resulting materials in his/her portfolio for the limited purpose of demonstrating his/her work to his/her prospective clients.

The agent shall produce work that contains no libelous or unlawful material that may cause harm or injury; that does not infringe upon or violate any copyright, trademark or other right or the privacy of others. The agent shall hold Silverleaf harmless against all liability, including expenses and reasonable counsel fees, from any claim which if sustained would constitute a breach of the foregoing warranties.

AGREED and ACCEPTED:

_____

Agent signature and date

_____

Agent name (print)

_____

Agent Address

_____

Agent phone number
Restrictions:

The above is a sample of a generic second shooter contract. You'll notice the area at the bottom has a line for 'restrictions' with space to add any specific restrictions for the agent's use of the pictures that they take.

Next is a questionnaire to give to any prospective clients, if you'd like to gather more info in order to give them a detailed price quote.

You can send this type of questionnaire to them via email, and have them fill it out and bring it with them to the consultation.

Alternatively, you can keep this list of questions on hand to ask a potential client at your first consultation.

I'm writing it out as a list of questions. If you will be sending it to your clients, you can create your own format with lines for the clients to write their answers on.

Wedding Client Questionnaire
Bride's name, Groom's name, contact email/phone#, Address, Do you have a wedding website? How long have you been together? How did you meet? Have you set a wedding date? Ceremony and reception venue? Time of ceremony? Do you have a wedding planner? What is the style or theme of your wedding? What is your budget? How many hours of coverage will you need? Are there multiple locations? Will you be doing a first look? Where will the couple's photos take place after the ceremony? Are you interested in a bridal session?

Model Release Form
As a resource for photography-related legal documents, Rachel Brenke at **www.thelawtog.com** is the best! Right now she's offering a free contract download.
www.rocketlawyer.com is another great resource for legal forms, including model release forms. You can sign up for a free one-week trial, or pay $5 per form.
Here's an example of a simple version of the standard model release form:

Effective as of the date shown below, approval for present and future use is being granted to _____(your business name) to use photographs and/or videos taken on _____(date) of _____(the photographed party).
The model is an adult and is fully authorized to sign this release.

For value received, the model grants consent to _____ (your company) and authorizes the use of any photographs taken of them, and any form and any media whatsoever, and the use of them to publicize, promote, and advertise.

The model hereby releases any and all claims in connection with the use of their photograph and its reproduction.

The model also agrees to the use of their name, or any fictitious name that may be chosen in connection with the photographs.

The model hereby waives any rights to inspect or approve the marketing materials that may be used in connection with their photographs, or the use to which it may be applied.

The model warrants that he/she is the undersigned and that he/she has read this release prior to the signing of this document.

Model's name_____date_____

You'll notice that this contract mentions the model granting their consent in exchange for 'value received'. This means that you must compensate them in some way for their participation. You can offer an 8x10 print, a disc of several watermarked images, or pay them to model for you.

Wedding day Timeline

This is going to vary quite a bit depending on how much time the client has hired you to shoot, what time of day it will be (morning or evening) and what type of wedding they're having. But it's a good idea to go over the timeline with your bride and come up with one that's customized for them.
Here's an example of a wedding with 8 hours of coverage:

Arrive at 10:00am – Details (dress, ring, shoes, flowers, jewelry)
10:30am – Getting ready (hair and makeup)
11:15am – Bride and Groom individual portraits
12:00pm – First look, couple portraits
12:45pm – Wedding party, family and friends
3:00pm – Ceremony
3:45pm – Couple Shots (during cocktail hour)
4:00-6:00pm – Reception

Wedding Shot List
This is a jumping-off point, add or subtract as needed to customize this and make it your own!
   Getting ready:
- Bride having hair styled and makeup applied
- Bride's gown hanging up or draped over chair
- Bride's shoes and jewelry
- Bride's and bridesmaid's bouquets
- Candid shots of bridesmaids getting dressed
- Mother of bride buttoning or lacing bride's dress
- Full-length shot of bride in gown, looking in mirror
- Bridesmaids reacting to seeing bride in gown
- Father of bride seeing bride in her gown
- Groom getting ready with groomsmen
- Groom's wedding band, cufflinks, shoes, tie, etc...
- Groomsmen putting on boutonnieres or ties

- Bride and groom leaving for first look
- First look, from bride's and groom's perspective
- Bride and groom together (couple portraits)
- Bridal party: Bride with maid of honor
- Bride with all bridesmaids individually
- Bride and all her bridesmaids together
- Bride and flower girl
- Same photos with groom and groomsmen/best man/ring bearer
- Bride and groom with entire bridal party

Ceremony:
- Interior and exterior of venue
- Groom walking down aisle with his mother
- Both sets of grandparents walking down aisle
- Groom waiting for bride
- Bridal party walking down aisle
- Bride and her father/escort walking down aisle
- Bride's father giving her away
- Bride and groom together
- Both sets of parents watching ceremony
- Wide shot of the ceremony from the back
- Wide shot of the guests from the front
- Candle lighting or other special moments
- Close-up of bride and groom during vows
- Close-up of their hands when they exchange rings
- The kiss!
- Newlyweds facing the guests
- Bride and groom hugging family
- Bride showing her ring to bridesmaids
- Bride and groom leaving the ceremony venue

The Family Formals:
- Bride and groom together
- Bride with mother

- Bride with Father
- Bride with both parents
- Bride with grandparents
- Bride with her entire immediate family
- Groom with mother
- Groom with father
- Groom with both parents
- Groom with grandparents
- Groom with his entire immediate family
- Bride and groom with bride's family
- Bride and groom with groom's family
- Bride and groom with both sets of parents
- Bride and groom with both sets of grandparents

The Reception:
- Interior and exterior shots of the venue
- Place cards, menus, centerpieces, decorations etc...
- The cake
- Hors d'oeuvres and specialty drinks
- Guests signing the guest book
- Bride and groom arriving
- Friends and family making toasts
- Bride and groom talking to guests
- Bride and groom's first dance
- Bride dancing with her father
- Groom dancing with his mother
- Parents and grandparents dancing
- Wedding party dancing
- Musicians, DJ and/or entertainers performing
- Guests dancing
- Bride and groom cutting the cake
- Bouquet toss
- Garter toss
- Newlywed's vehicle
- Bride and groom leaving the reception

Print Release Form
This can be printed out and inserted into a CD case, or you can save it as a digital file and include it with the digital photos on a disc or thumb drive.

I, (your name), of (Your business name) am the rightful copyright owner of these digital images. I authorize the owner of this disk the right to print these files. Original copyright remains with the photographer. The photos may be printed but not altered or edited in any way other than by the photographer. Any alterations are a violation of the copyright.

(Your business name) is not liable for print quality, cropping or coloring of any photos not printed directly through my professional lab. Photo quality is only guaranteed for photos purchased directly through me and my lab.

Proper recognition of (Your business name) is appreciated and requested when publishing photos and using them online. Photos may not be entered into any contests without my prior consent.

What to include in your contract:
As always, you should have a lawyer in your area look over any contract forms that you plan to use. This is simply an example.

This agreement is entered into between:
Bride's name_____
Groom's name_____
(Hereinafter referred to as "the client")
AND
(Your name)
(Your business name)

(Your address)
(Your phone number)
(Your email address)
(Hereinafter referred to as "the photographer")

1. The client hereby engages the photographer to cover the marriage of the client on the _____ day of _____ 20____ for a fee of $_____ (_____) inclusive of all taxes.

2.The scope of the photography coverage is detailed in the Wedding Photography Checklist which is annexed hereto and forms part of this contract.

3.The client agrees to pay the photographer's fee on the following terms:

     3.1 A retainer of $_____ upon signing of this agreement and the balance of $_____ on or before the _____ day of _____ 20____.

     3.2 Additional charges for extra photography time on the wedding day shall be charged at $_____ per hour, and shall become payable within 14 days of presentation of an invoice by the photographer.

4. The client agrees that the retainer is non-transferable and non-refundable in the event of a cancellation by the client.

5. The client agrees that this agreement shall be deemed cancelled if all monies are not paid on time as stipulated above and the photographer shall have no further obligations to the client.

6. The photographer shall retain copyright in all material produced by the photographer and this right shall accrue to the benefit of his/her successors, legal representatives and assigns.

7. The photographer grants the client the right to make unlimited number and format of copies of the photographs in nay medium for personal use. The client shall obtain written permission from the photographer prior to selling or publishing any of the material for financial gain.

8. The client grants the photographer and his/her successors the unrestricted right to use and alter the material for commercial, promotional, marketing, competition or other purposes without compensation and hereby release and shall hold harmless the photographer and his/her successors from all claims or liability resulting from the use of the material.

Client's signatures:
Signed by the Bride on this _____day of _____ 20___
Signature_____
Signed by the Groom on this _____day of _____ 20__
Signature_____

Photographer's signature:
Signed on this_____day of _____ 20_____
Signature_____

You'll notice that clause 7 is basically a print release, so if you won't be allowing your clients to print their own photos you'll want to leave that out.

Clause 8 is an abbreviated model release, giving you right to use the images in any way you choose. This is a simpler option to having them sign an additional model release form.

It can be helpful to go over each point with your clients, and have them initial after each clause.

The actual contract that I use is somewhat different from the one above, with several additional clauses that I've added. I have a clause that state's my clients are familiar with my style and they acknowledge that they may not reject the photos based on taste or esthetic criteria.

Another clause explains that I will do my best to capture all the photos that the clients want, but due to circumstances beyond my control that may not be possible, and there will be no refunds or discounts in that case.

I also add that I provide JPEG images only, and RAW files are not provided.

After one "interesting" wedding I added a clause that if I or my assistant feel threatened or harassed, or are in physical danger that we reserve the right to leave without issuing a refund.

You can see that you'll need to alter or expand on this basic contract to fit your needs, and it will most likely change over time.

In the second clause above, you'll notice I referred to a Wedding Photography Checklist. I attach that to the contract, and it basically provides me with the contact information I need.

On that sheet, I have spaces for the following:
- Bride's name and address, cell# and email
- Groom's name and address, cell# and email
- Address of the home or hotel where the bride will get ready
- What time I will arrive there
- If they will be having a first look or not
- Time and location of first look
- Time and location of pre-wedding photos
- Ceremony location (street address) and time of ceremony
- Reception address and time it starts
- Name and cell# of their wedding coordinator

I also attach a sheet that details the terms of the wedding collection that they have chosen. This lists the price, and all it includes.

There is also a sheet with a delivery schedule, that tells them how long after the wedding they should expect to receive the online gallery, album, prints, and digital images.

I tell the bride that I'll put a sneak peek online within three days, but I'll make sure to have one up within 24 hours. The online gallery is ready within 2 weeks, the digital files and prints within 4 weeks, and any albums no later than 6 weeks.

I know these pages haven't covered everything that you'll need in your business, but I hope you'll find enough to get started and start growing!

I wish I could watch over your shoulder and cheer you on as you begin this adventure, and I wish you all the best! Here's to many years of success for you and your business!

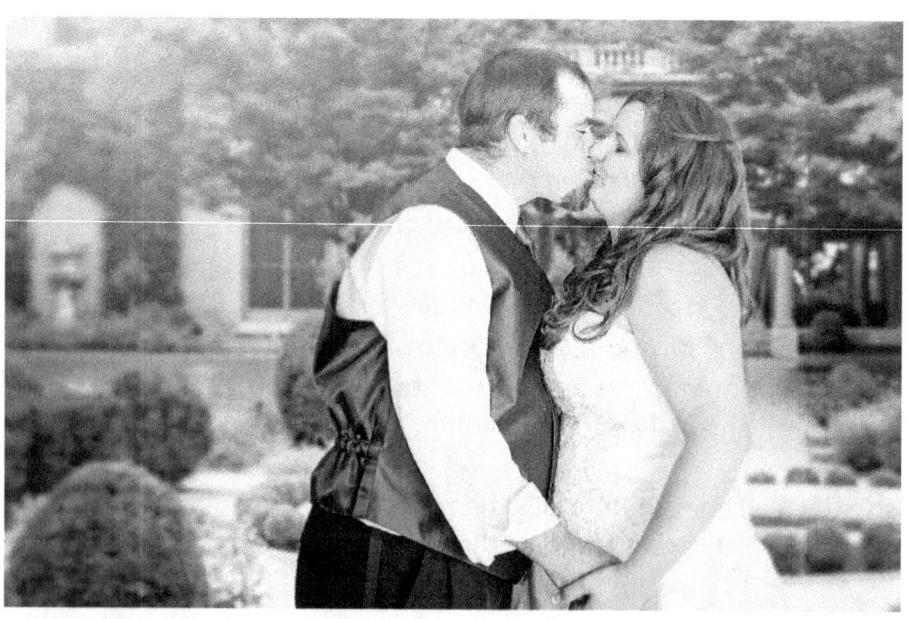

The following pages are more wedding photos that I couldn't bear to leave out! Enjoy!

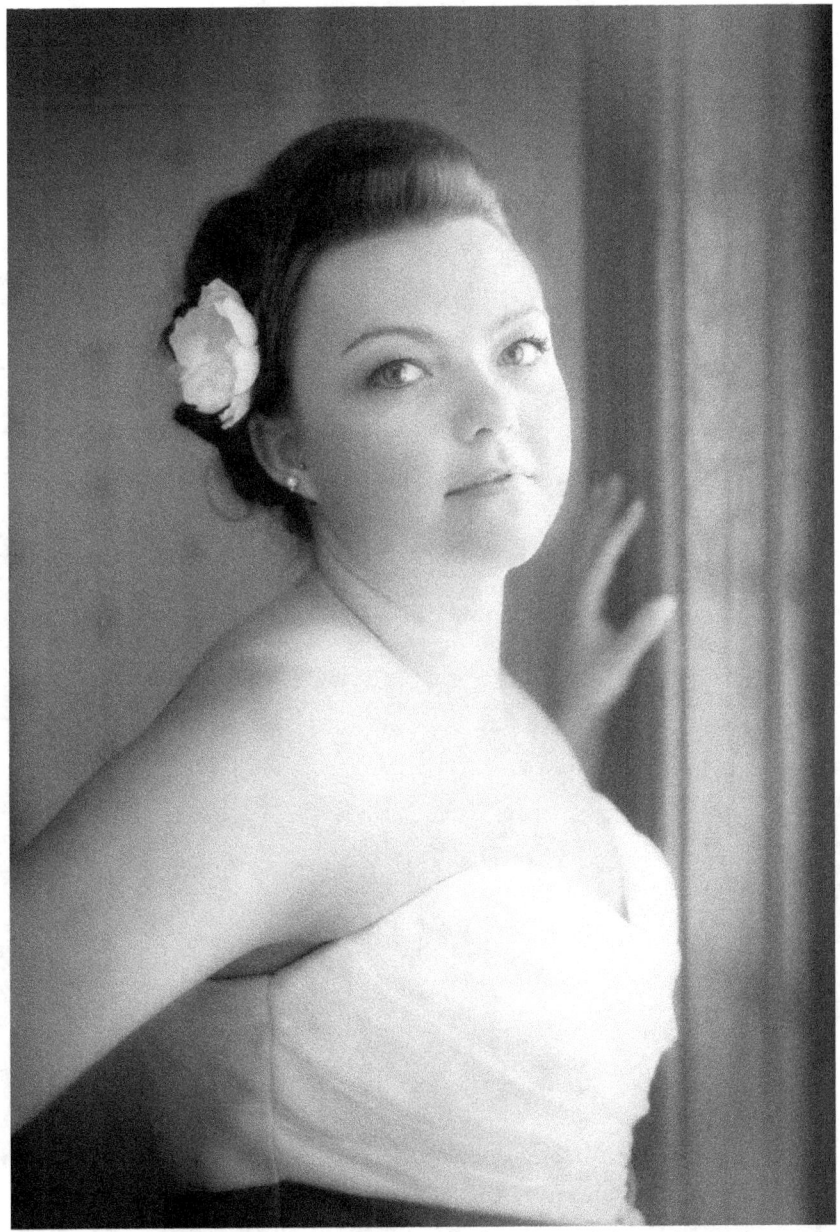

Natural light from a window is the first thing I look for.

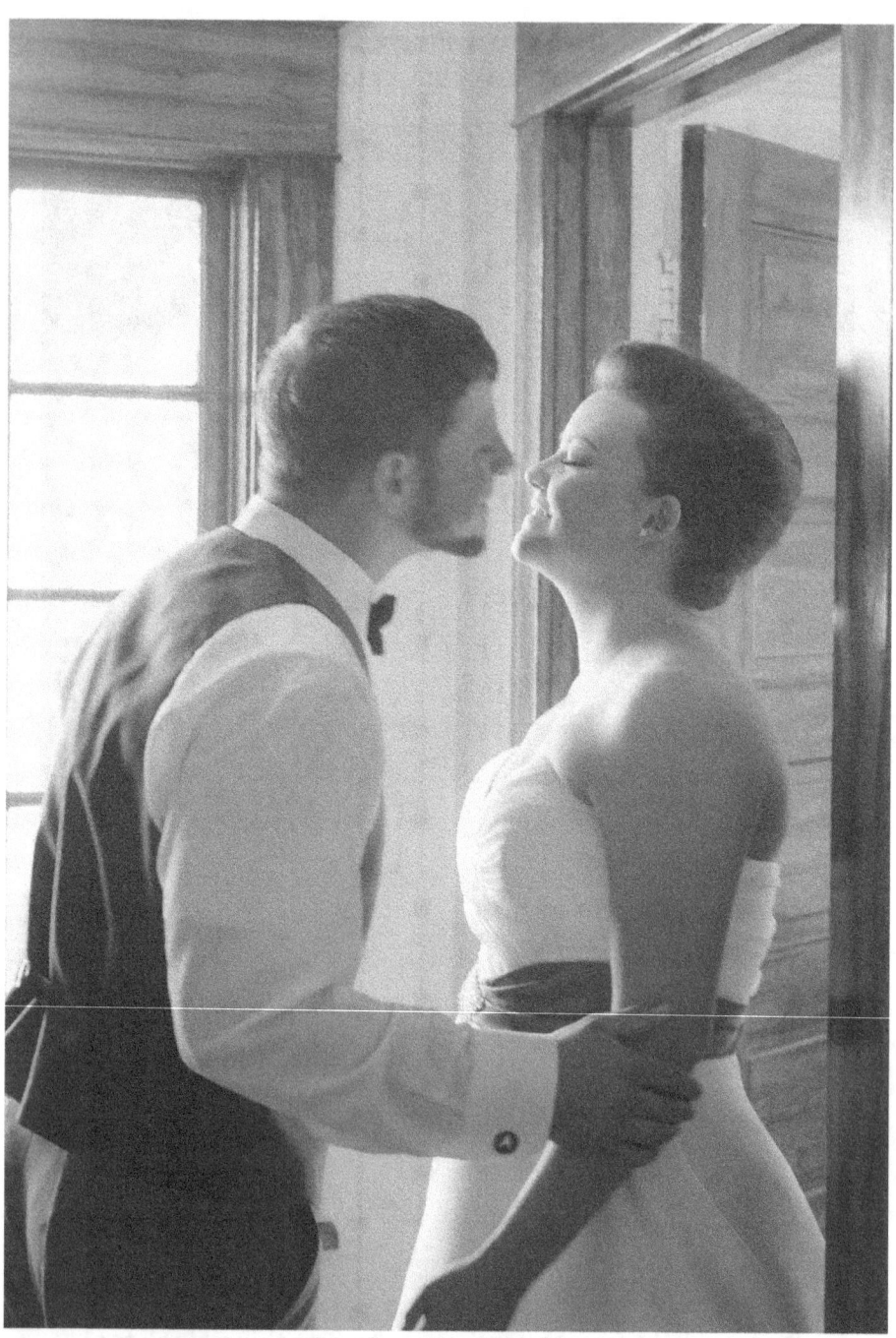

Indoor First Look

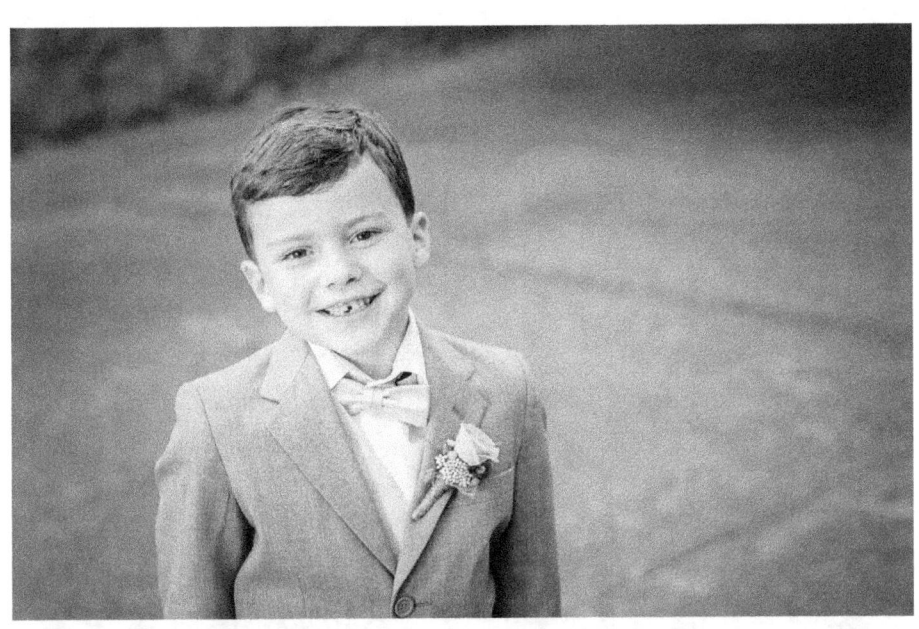

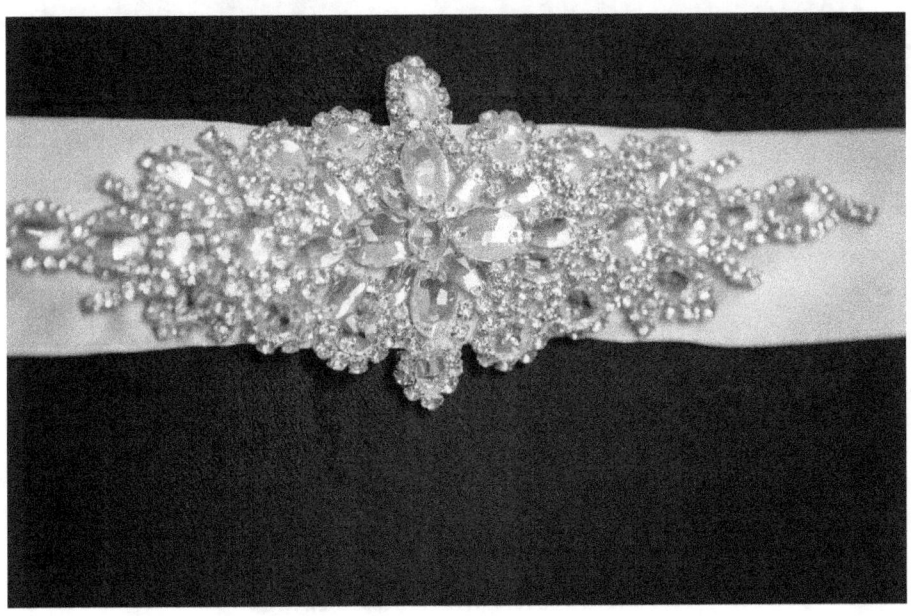

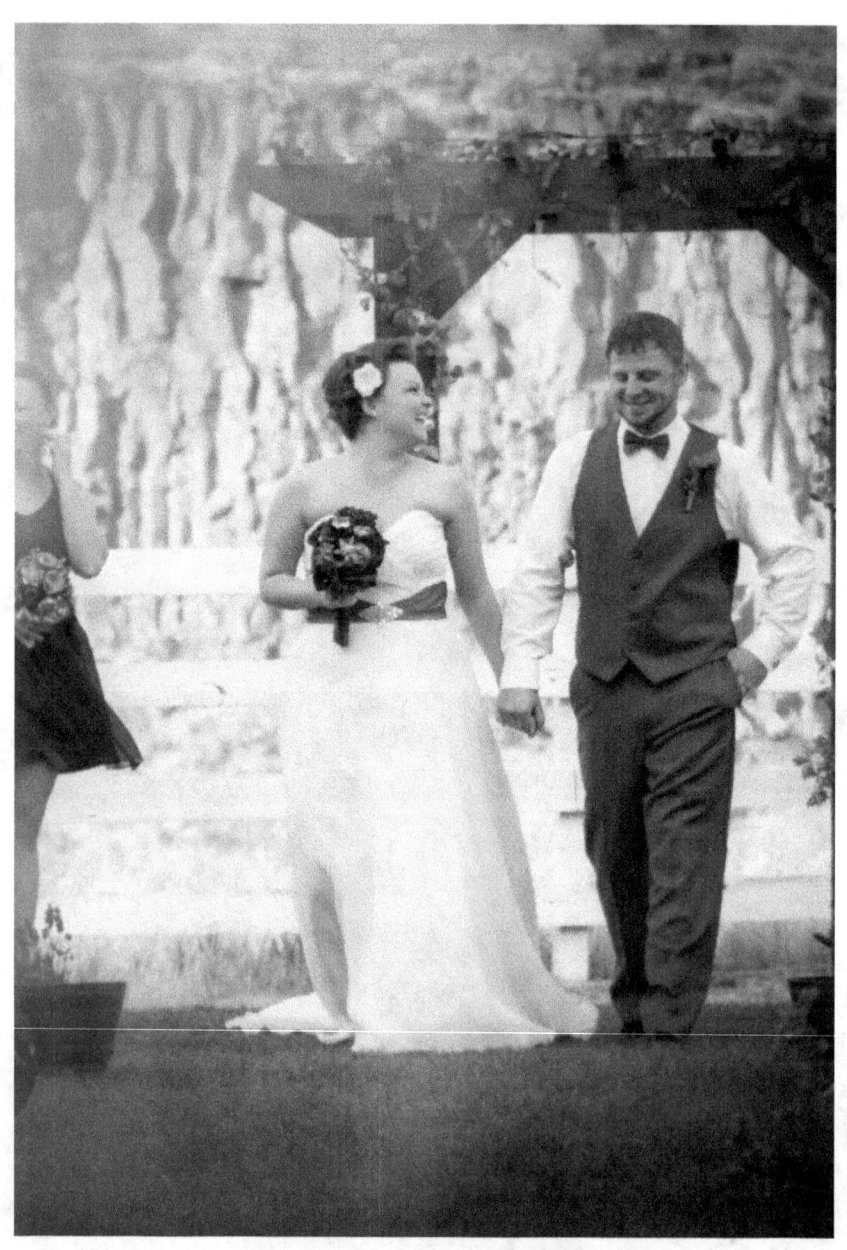

The Newly Married Couple

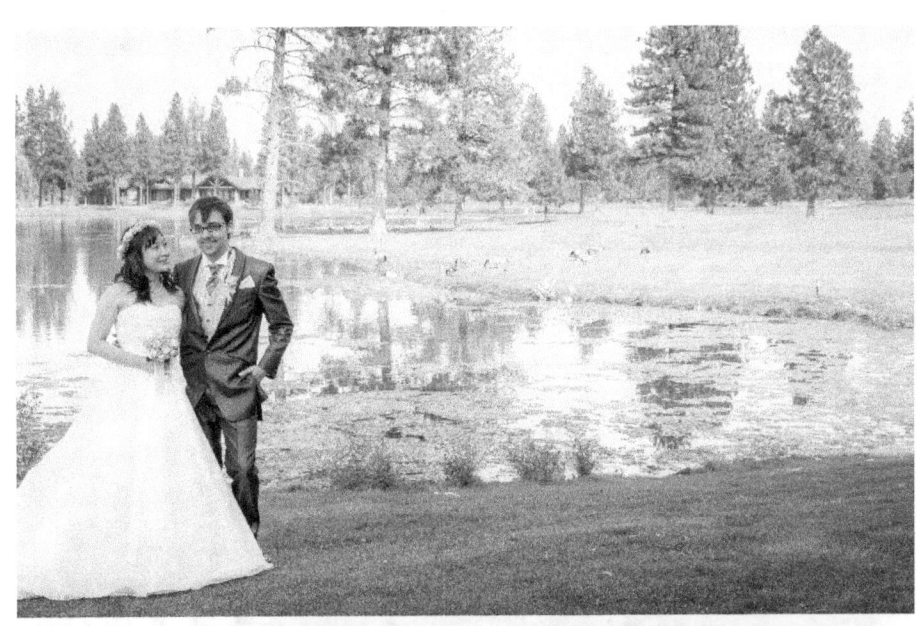

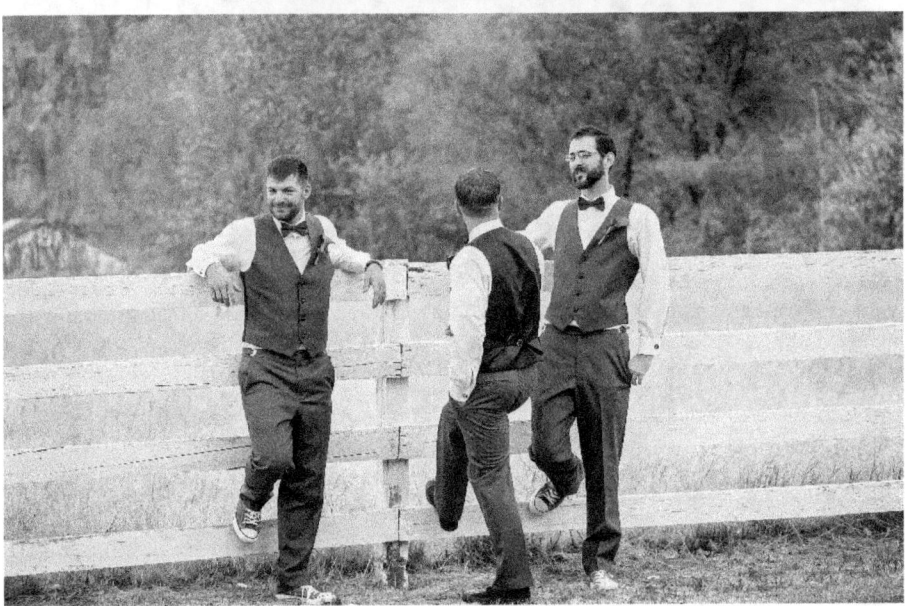

Candid Moments

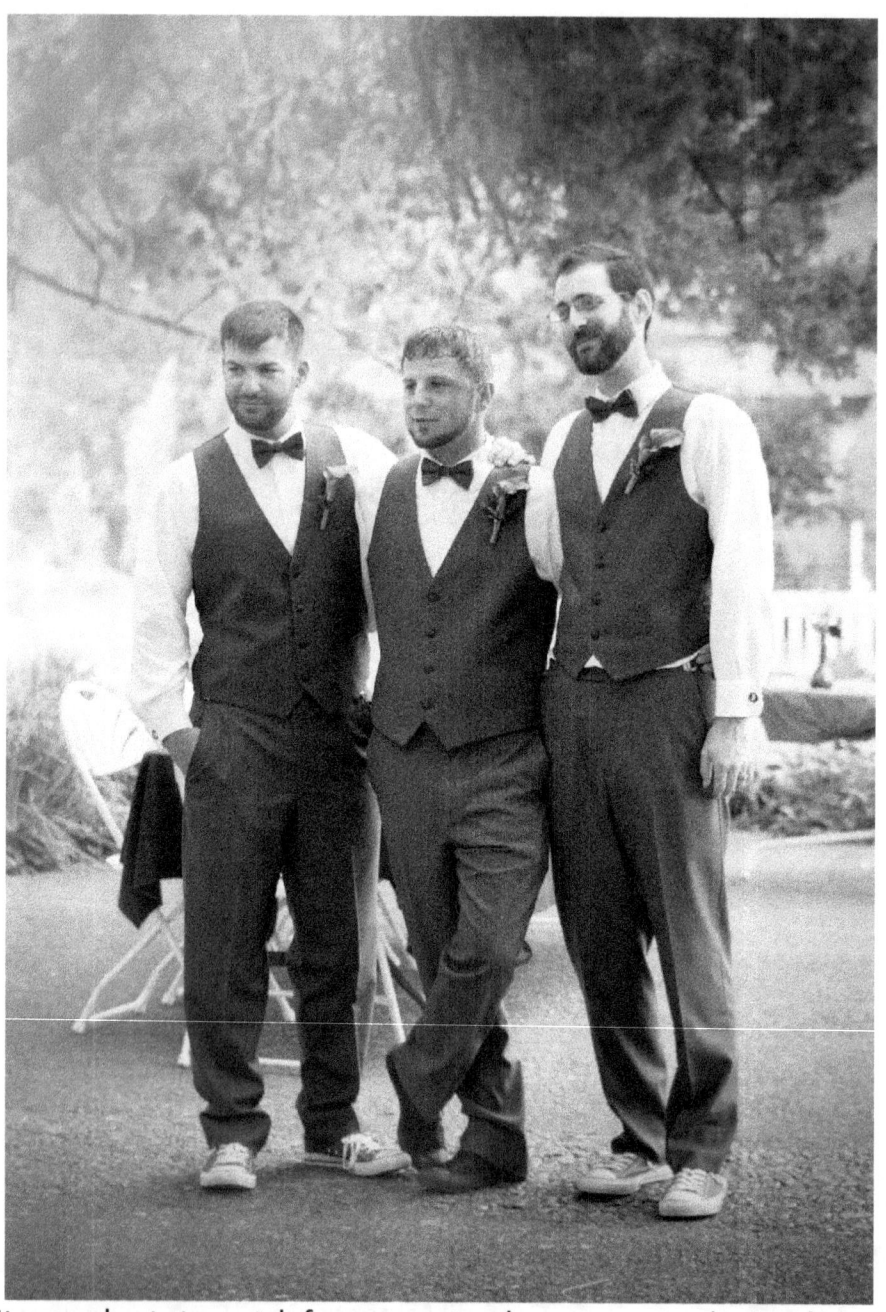

It never hurts to watch for moments when someone else is taking a picture!

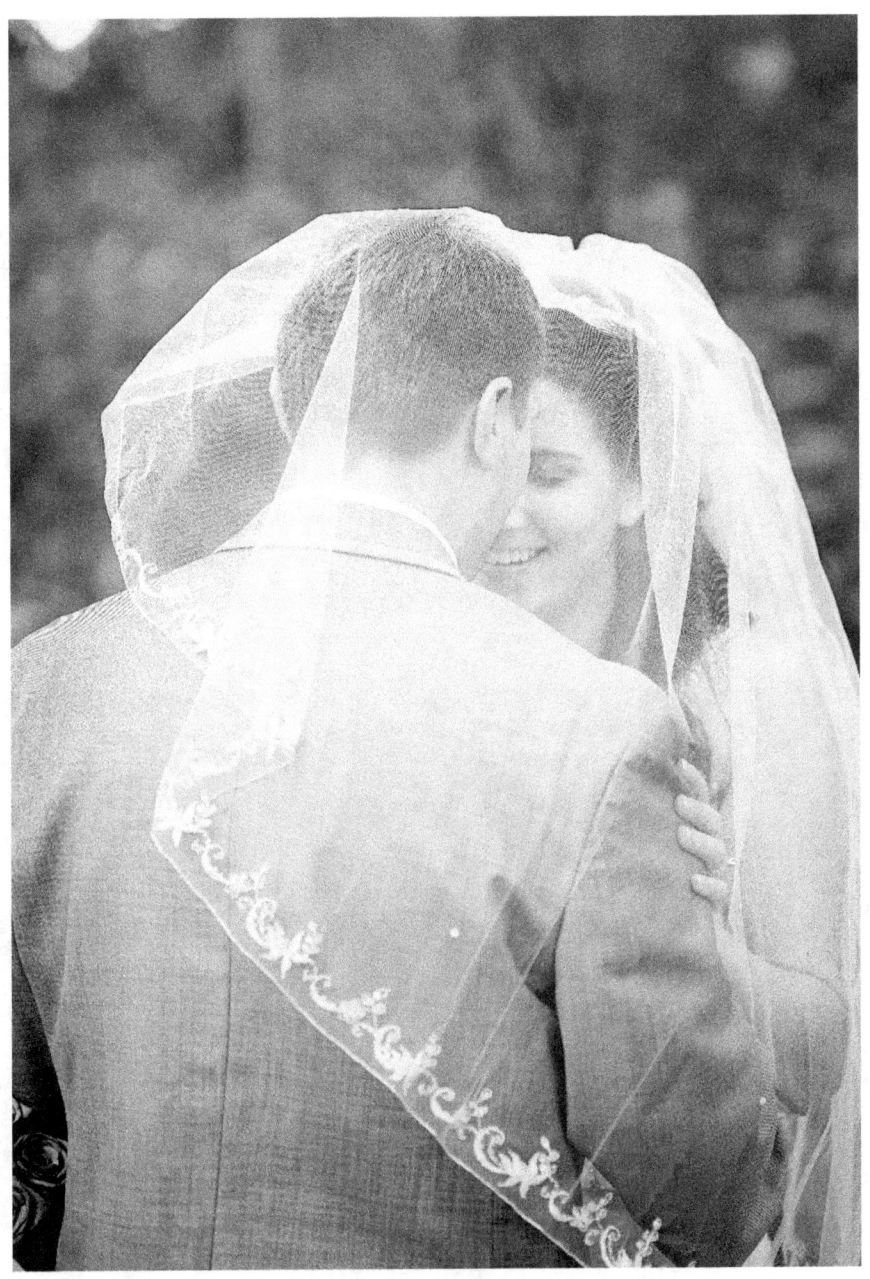

If your bride has a veil, use it for some romantic images of the couple.

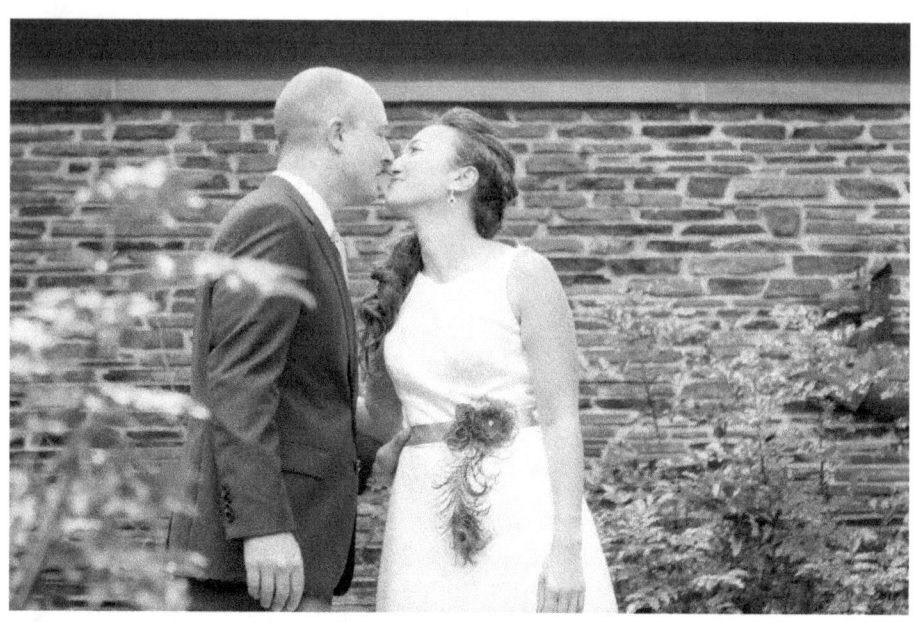

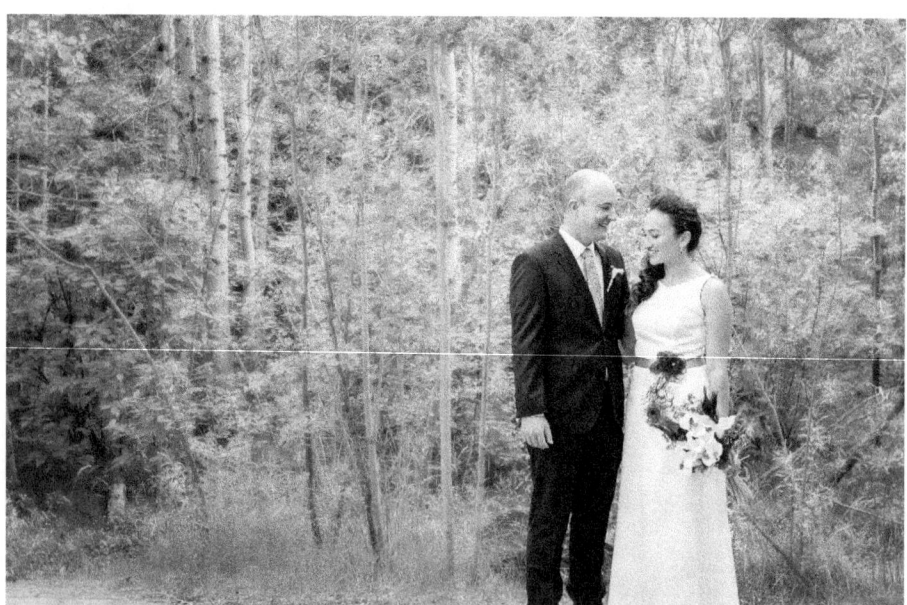

Look for a variety of backgrounds at the venue.

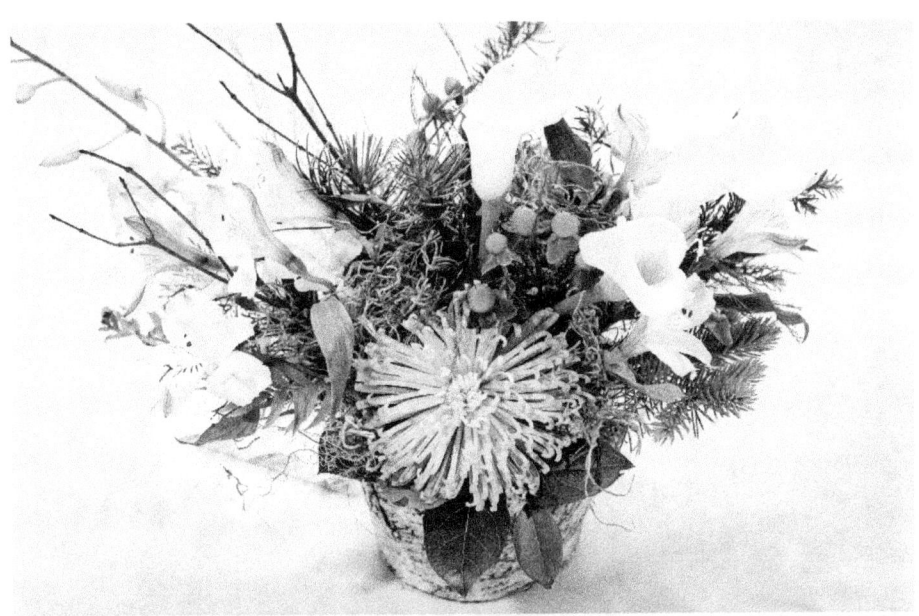

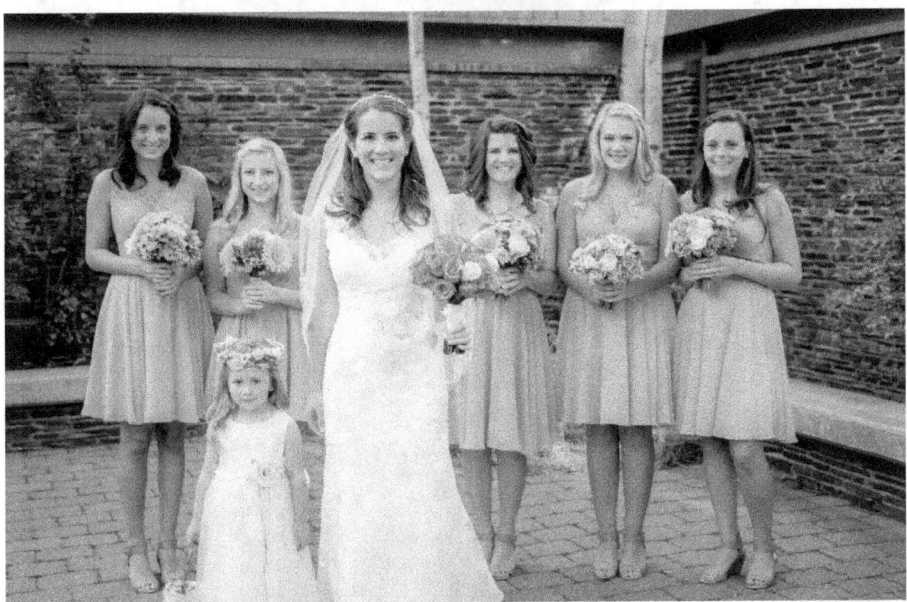

Flowers add a great touch, don't forget to have the ladies hold their bouquets in the bridal party pictures.

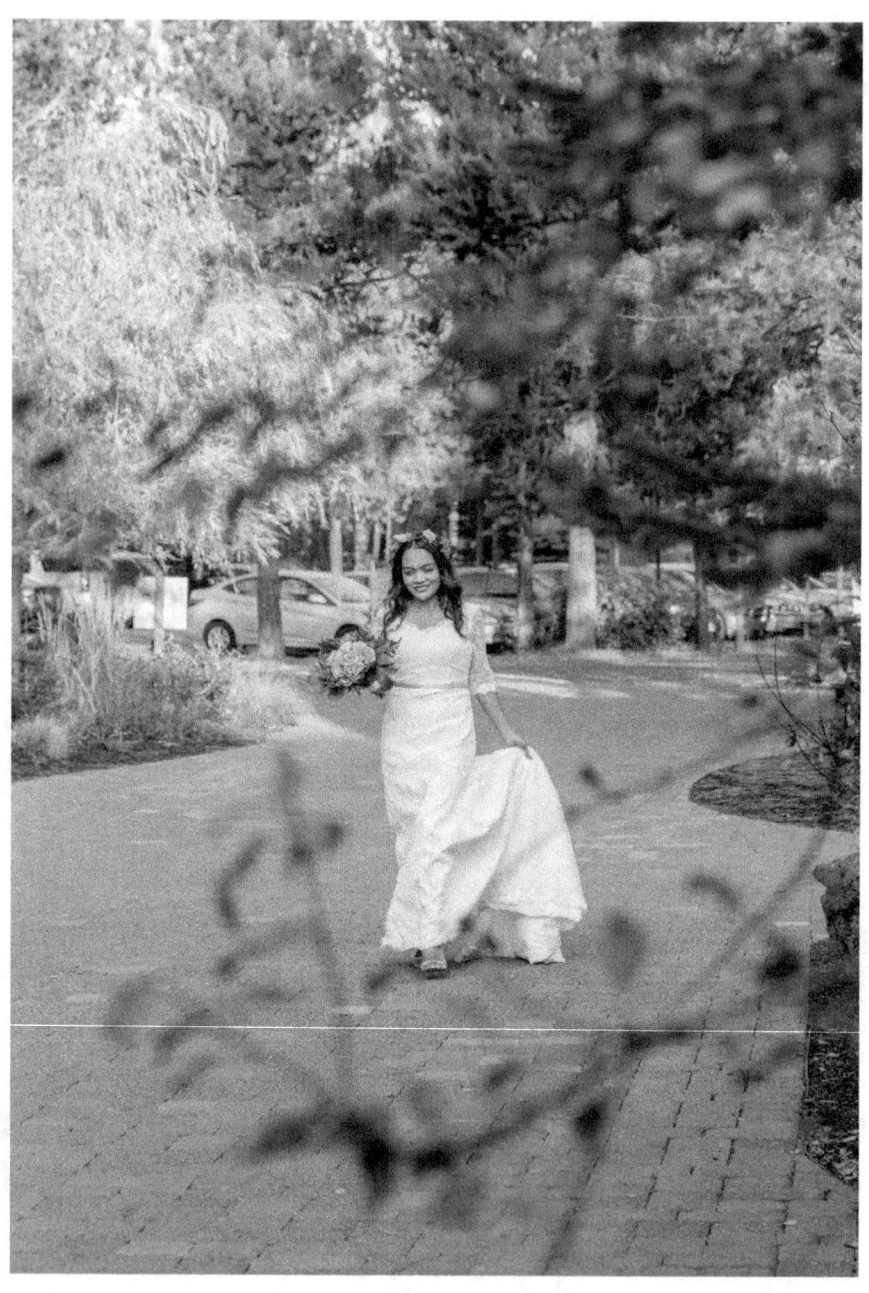

Arriving at the venue before the bride will let you photograph her arrival.

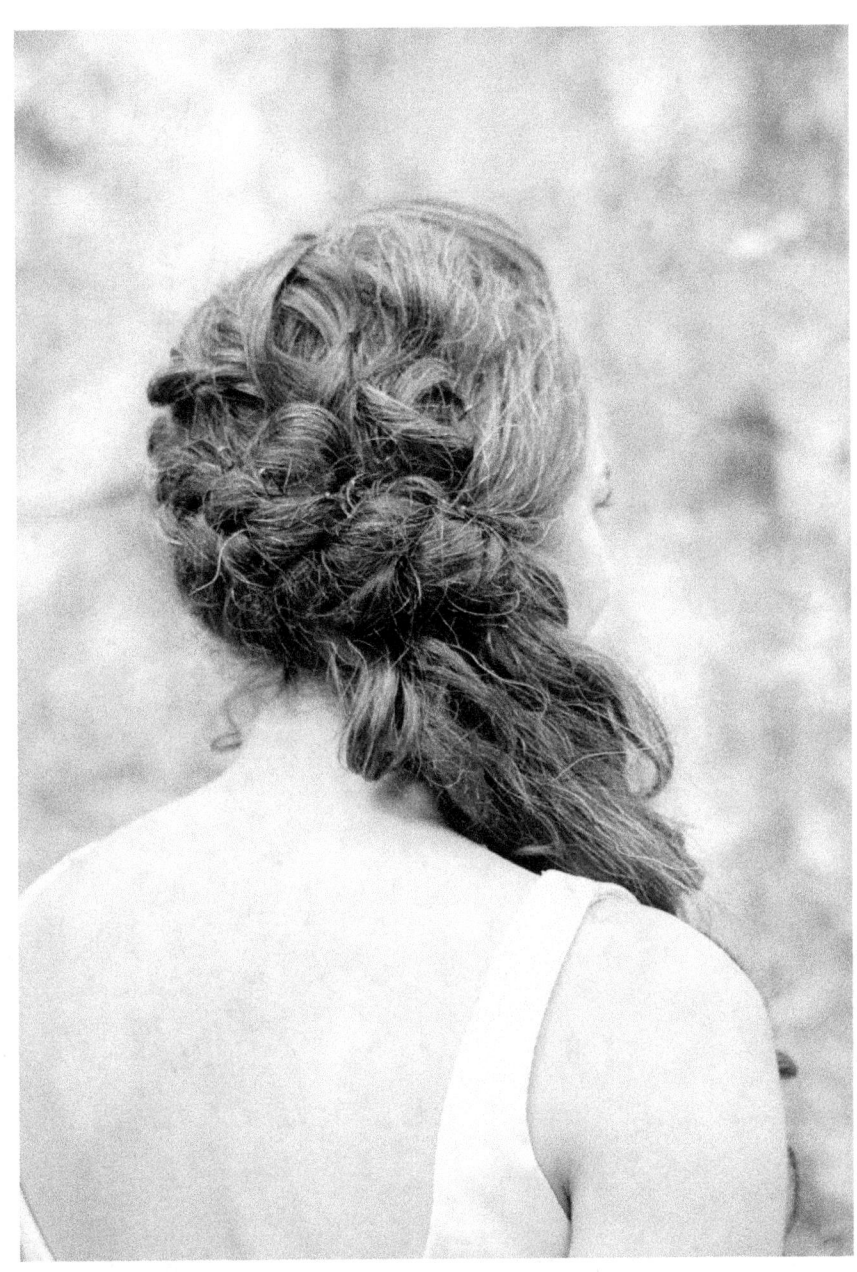

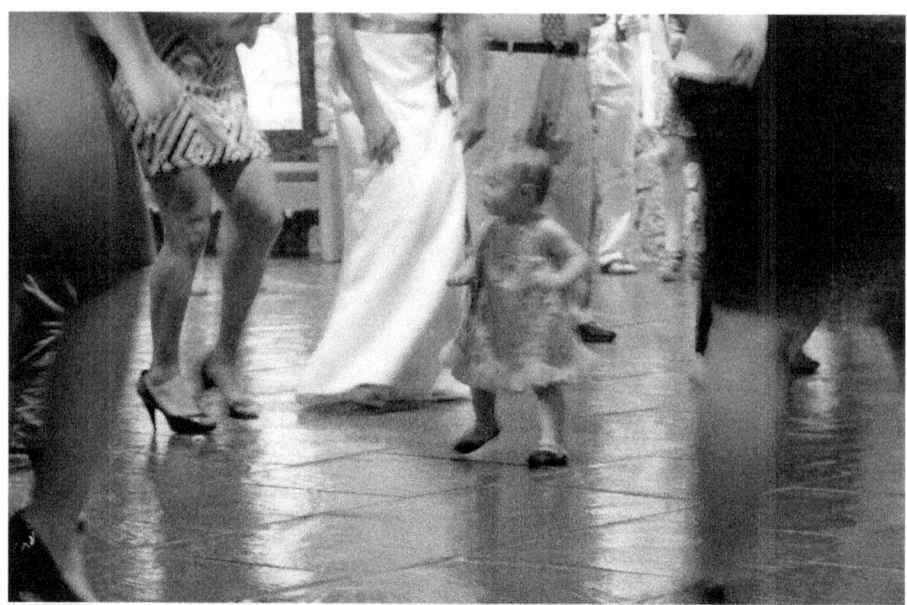

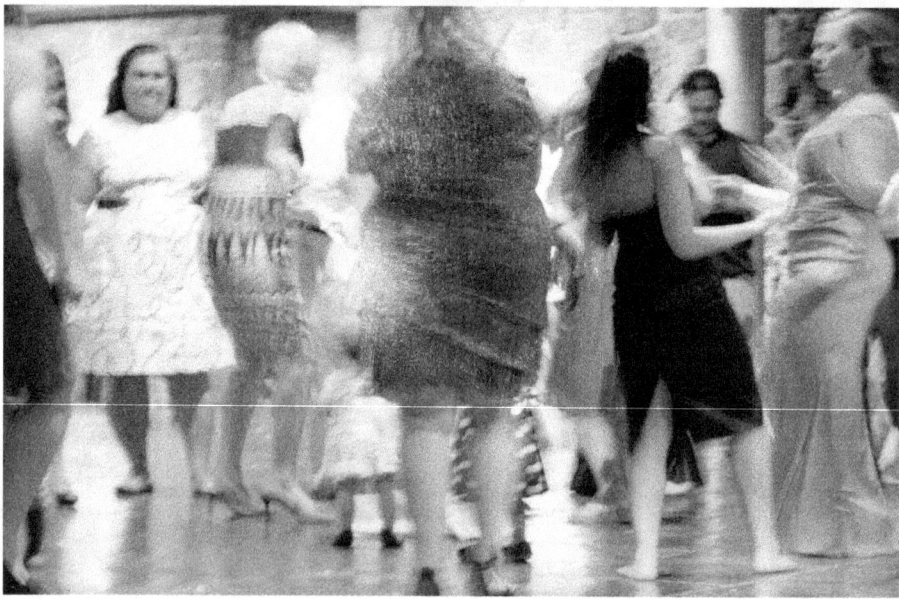

These are the 'blurry' dance images from that early wedding. I'm including these to show you how *not* to shoot a reception. ☺

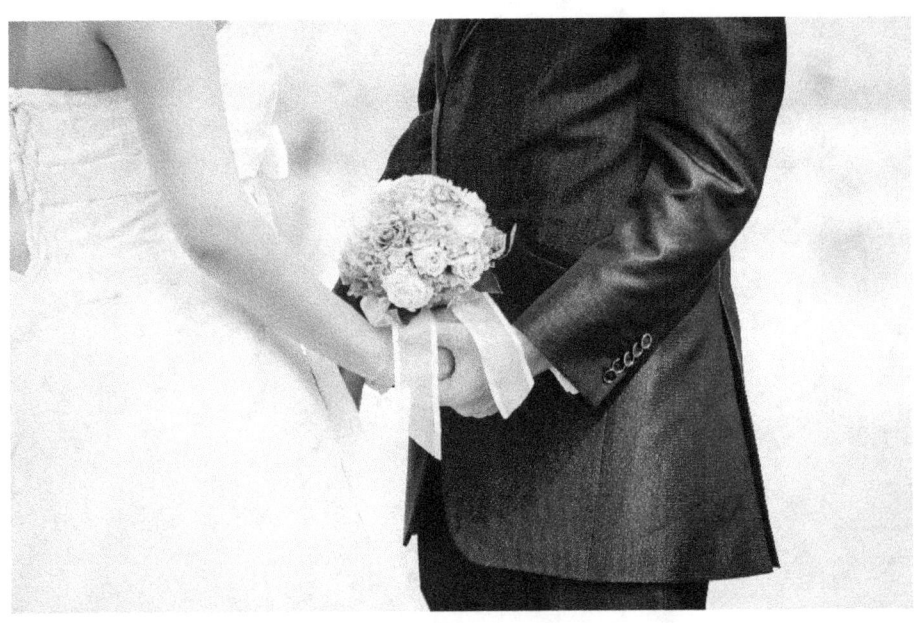

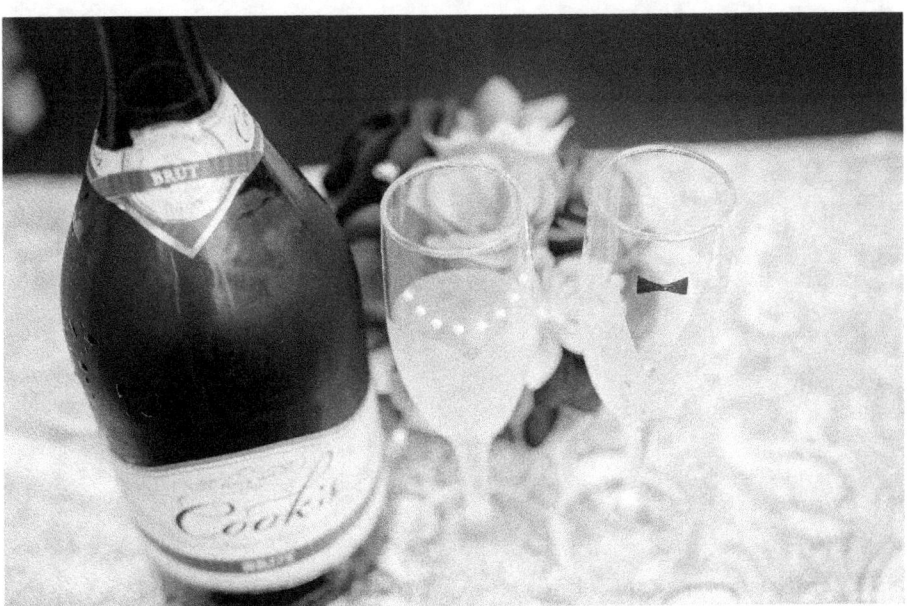

More lovely detail shots! These champagne glasses had been made for the couple by a close friend.

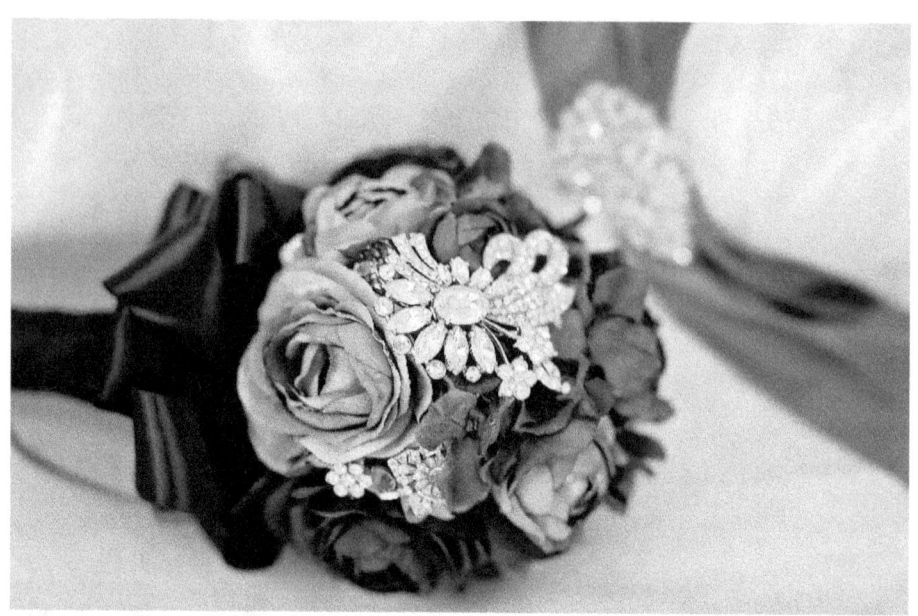

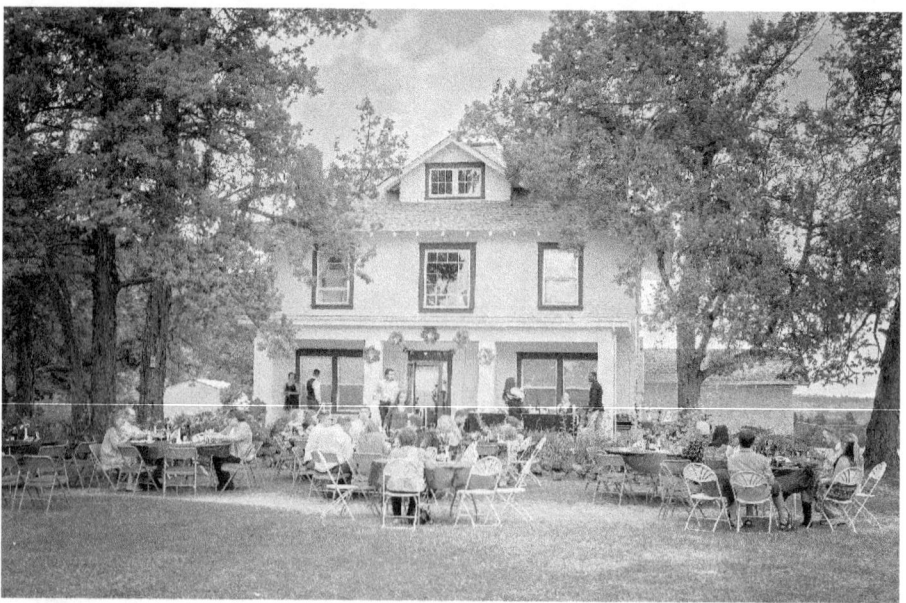

Make sure to include the entire venue in a few shots.

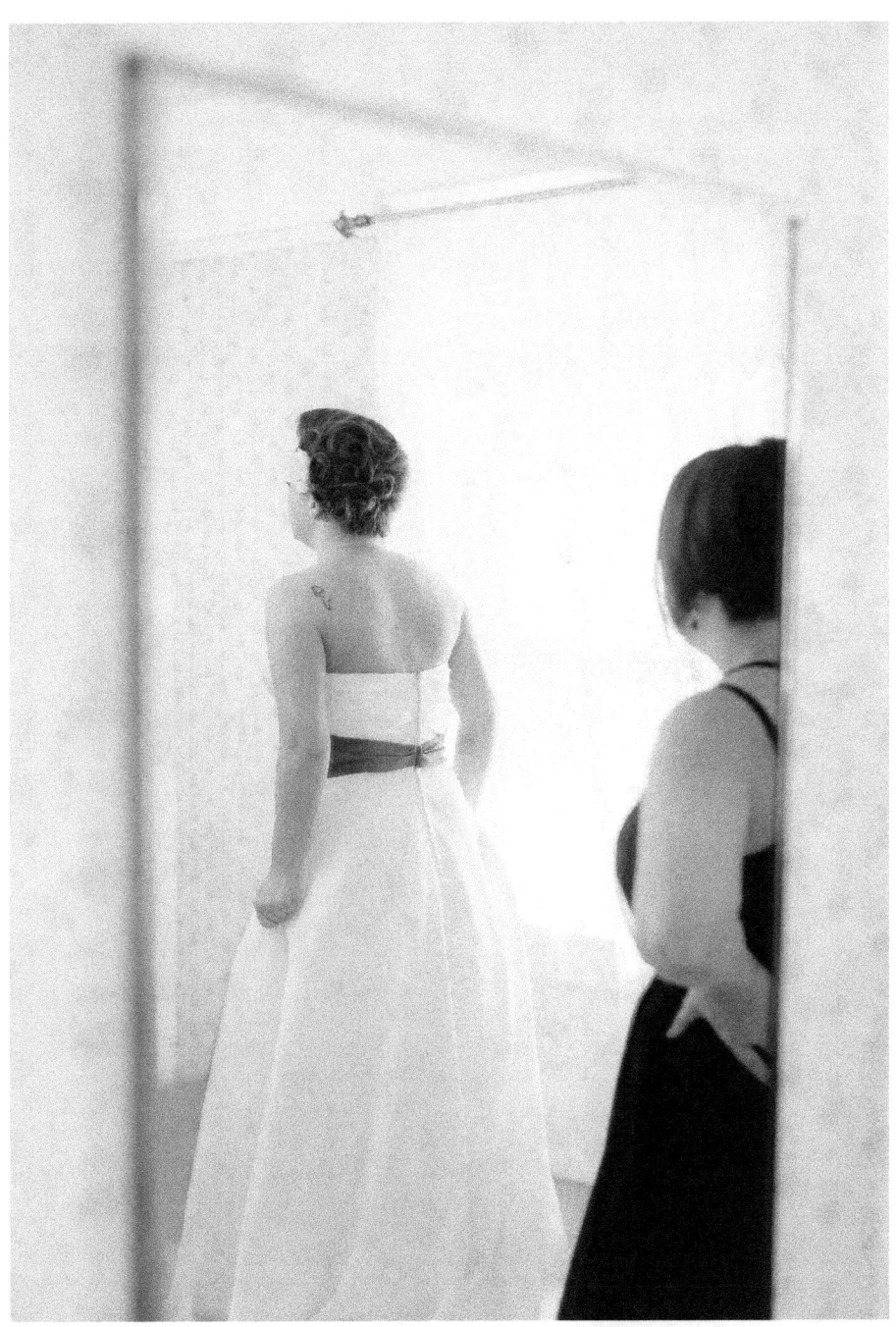

Using a mirror doesn't have to always show the front view of people.

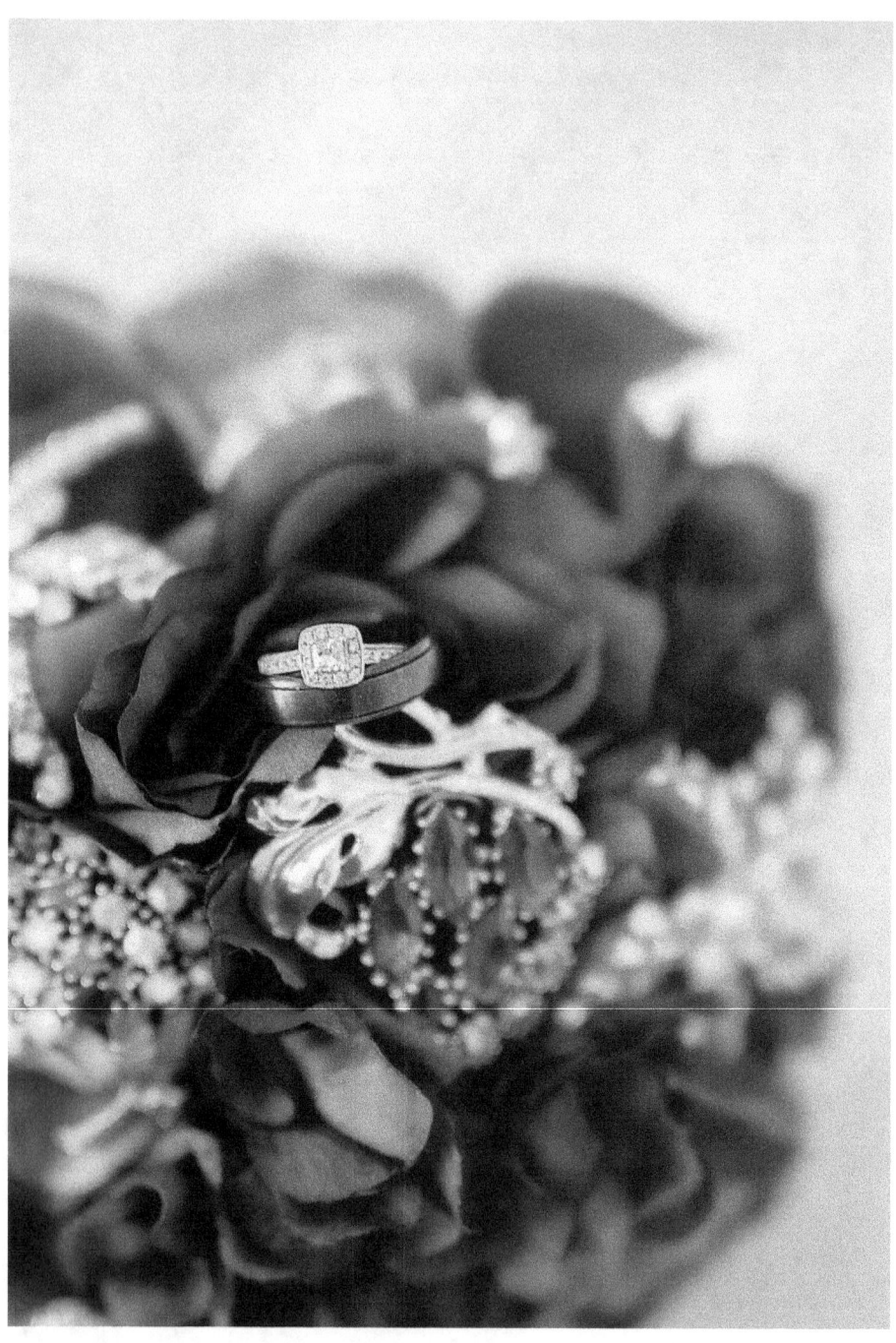

(I don't know about you, but I love to write in my books! I thought
I'd include a few pages for notes.)

~ Notes ~

~ Notes ~

~ Notes ~

~ Notes ~

~ Notes ~